M000208443

JOY
FOR ALL
Seasons

JOY FOR ALL Seasons

Carol Burton McLeod

BRIDGE LOGOS

Newberry, FL 32669

Bridge Logos, Inc.
Newberry, FL 32669

Joy For All Seasons
By Carol Burton McLeod

Copyright ©2016 by Bridge Logos, Inc.

All rights reserved. Under International Copyright Law, no part of the publication may be reproduced, stored, or transmitted by any means—electronic, mechanical, photographic (photocopy), recording, or otherwise—without written permission from the Publisher.

Printed in the United States of America.

Library of Congress Catalog Card Number: 2016937556

International Standard Book Number: 978-1610361569 Paperback
International Standard Book Number: 978-1610360692 Hardcover

Unless otherwise noted, all Scripture quotations are from the New American Standard Bible (NASB). NEW AMERICAN STANDARD BIBLE®, Copyright © 1960,1962, 1963,1968,1971,1972,1973,1975,1977,1995 by The Lockman Foundation. Used by permission

The Message. Copyright © 1993, 1994, 1995, 1996, 2000, 2001, 2002. Used by permission of NavPress Publishing Group

NIV are taken from THE HOLY BIBLE, NEW INTERNATIONAL VERSION®, NIV® Copyright © 1973, 1978, 1984, 2011 by Biblica, Inc.® Used by permission. All rights reserved worldwide.

08-02-16

Dedication

This Book is Lovingly Dedicated to:
Carolyn Ashcraft Hogan

My mentor, role model and life-long friend.

You have taught me how to live a life of constant devotion to Christ.

You have taught me how to simply rest in His presence.

You have taught me the value of doing life on my knees.

Thank you, Carolyn, for showing me that there truly is Joy for all seasons of life!

Endorsements

Have you ever wondered if it's possible to choose joy in every situation? In Joy For All Seasons you will discover how to trust God when life isn't fair, how to ponder Scripture that will transform your thinking, and how to develop a daily pattern for turning disappointment and hurt into a heart that rejoices in the middle of uncertainty. You'll discover it's okay to ask God the hard questions—but you'll also learn to immediately seek answers in His truth! Carol McLeod has done a masterful job of pointing us to abiding joy in the middle of life's harsh realities. Buy one copy of this book for yourself and ten more to give to your friends.

— **CAROL KENT**, SPEAKER AND BEST-SELLING AUTHOR
OF *WHEN I LAY MY ISAAC DOWN* (NAVPRESS)

Carol McLeod knows grief and depression first-hand -- but more importantly, she knows the secret to moving through dark valleys where jubilant joy lights up our lives. In both poetic and practical ways, Joy For All Seasons *takes us from despair to delight using a simple plan, proven to break our chains of emotional bondage. No matter what season you are in, you will benefit from reading this healing devotional.*

— **ANITA AGERS BROOKS**, INSPIRATIONAL BUSINESS/LIFE COACH,
INTERNATIONAL SPEAKER AND AWARD-WINNING AUTHOR
OF *GETTING THROUGH WHAT YOU CAN'T GET OVER,*
DEATH DEFIED, LIFE DEFINED: A MIRACLE MAN'S MEMOIR, AND
FIRST HIRED, LAST FIRED: HOW TO BECOME IRREPLACEABLE IN ANY JOB MARKET

In Joy For All Seasons *Carol's life giving spirit breathes hope and healing into a place of hopelessness and despair. Her words will leave you feeling inspired and empowered to live each and every day to the fullest.*

—SARAH MCLEAN, CEO OF PROJECT31 AND AUTHOR
OF *PINK IS THE NEW BLACK*

Get ready for a fresh wind of hope that lasts! With real and raw honesty, armed with practical, simple joy strategies, my friend Carol McLeod will show you how to shake off discouragement and enter into a new realm of lasting, true JOY!

—LYNETTE LEWIS, CORPORATE SPEAKER, CONSULTANT AND AUTHOR
OF *CLIMBING THE LADDER IN STILETTOS*

While facing a terrifying cancer journey, Carol McLeod lived what she has written - exuding joy, kindness and love. She knows from experience how to tap into the deep well of God's empowering joy. This book is encouraging, convicting and a must read!!

—CHERYL WEBER, CO-HOST OF "100 HUNTLEY STREET"

Table of Contents

Introduction

Did you ever wish that you could just have a cup of tea and an afternoon of conversation with a woman who just "gets you"?

Have you ever desired to dig deeply into the treasures of a woman's heart who has experienced many seasons of life?

Perhaps you desperately long to receive a strategy from a woman who has been to battle and has actually come out alive! Wouldn't it be wonderful to see the sparkle in her eyes, the spring in her step and the grin on her face in the season after the battle has ended?!

If those particular desires have lingered in your heart, perhaps by picking up this book, you have come to the right place! *Joy For All Seasons* is more than a memory book, it is richer than a stand-up conversation and it is certainly not a soliloquy. This book is a weekly devotional that will draw you into thoughtful prayer, vibrant change and, as always, turn your heart toward the Father.

You will see yourself in this book! You might even exclaim, "Why! I didn't know that anyone else felt like that!" But this is not a book chiefly about feelings; it is a call to allow your life to mirror the life of Jesus. It is a challenge to walk away from the mundane and from the ordinary. It is a loving invitation to be embraced in a life so rare and so compelling that even the angels stand to their feet and applaud.

My prayer for you as you read and meditate on these weekly devotions is that you will find that place of quiet rest that is unique only in the heart of God. Please take the time to incorporate the suggested Bible readings into your weekly readings. After all, it is not human words that actually matter ... it is only God's powerful words that will bring complete change and lasting comfort to your life.

Also, I do hope that you will take the time to answer the questions at the end of each devotional. This book is not just about me ... it is about you and I pursuing the heart and plan of God for our lives.

And finally, this book has been written in a style that is easy to share with others. I hope that you will use this book to facilitate conversations and sweet devotions with those whom you know the best and love the most.

And so, my new friend, as you immerse yourself in this book, this is my heartfelt prayer for you ...

"I am asking God to give you wise minds and spirits attuned to His will, and so acquire a thorough understanding of the ways in which God works.

I pray that you'll live well for the Master, making Him proud of you as you work hard in His orchard. As you learn more and more how God works, you will learn how to do your work.

I pray that you'll have the strength to stick it out over the long haul — not the grim strength of gritting your teeth but the glory-strength God gives. It is strength that endures the unendurable and spills over into joy, thanking the Father who makes us strong enough to take part in everything bright and beautiful that He has for us."

– COLOSSIANS 1:9–11 IN *THE MESSAGE BIBLE*

And I pray that whatever season of life you find yourself in today, you will discover the joy that only His presence provides!

With great joy —

Carol

Acknowledgements

The words "thank you" are the two most underused words in the human language. No matter how times those two words are written, spoken, whispered, shouted or sung, it is never enough.

And so … let me just say … to my family …

Thank you to my husband and love of my life, **Craig**, who endures unfolded laundry, messy bathrooms and countless meals from Panera while I am in the throes of completing a book. Thank you for cheering for me … for loving me … and for believing in me!

Thank you to my mom, **Joan Burton Ormanoski**, and her wonderful husband, **Leo**, for their companionship, love and prayers. I love being with both of you … our times together are never long enough!

Thank you to my mother-in-law, **Becky McLeod**, for her quiet spirit and steadfast prayers.

Thank you, **Matthew**, for being an outstanding man of honor and integrity. You are my first-born son and will always hold a special place in my heart. I always knew that you had the word "leader" tattooed on your very soul. Thank you for being an example to young men on and off the court. Thank you for loving Emily so completely and for building a family at which heaven smiles!

Thank you, **Christopher**, for enduring my phone calls when I ask you yet another technical question! Thank you for your kindness and patience with my never-ending list of computer problems! What joy you have always brought to my life! Thank you for singing the song that you were created to sing. Thank you for loving Liz with your whole heart and for being a daddy who reads, plays and prays.

Thank you, **Jordan**, for your mad production skills! Thank you for dreaming with me and for believing in your mom. I believe in you … more than you know. You are the answer to my prayers! Thank you for your wisdom and for your tenderness to all members of our family. Thank you for loving Allie and for being not only a wonderful father to Ian but also his best buddy.

Thank you, **Joy**, for your friendship and for your sweet spirit. I remember that when you were a little girl, for Christmas one year, you gave me a dish that had written on it, "A daughter is a little girl who grows up to be your friend." How true that is for me! You are one of my dearest friends. You light up every room with delight and joy! Thank you for loving your Chris!

Thank you, **Joni**, for dreaming big dreams and for obeying God's voice. No matter where life takes you, always remember that, "Home is where the Mom is!" You amaze me with your passion and with your dedication. I know that you will change the world! Know that no matter how far you travel, there is someone who is praying for you every single hour of every single day.

Thank you, **Emily**, for loving our Matt and for being a woman of virtue and faith. No one cooks like you do ... believes like you do ... or perseveres like you do! Thank you for great conversations and sweet Texas hospitality! Thank you for loving each one of the little McLeod's who are filling your home ... Olivia Mae, Wesley Eric, Roger Boyce and Elizabeth Joy.

Thank you, **Liz**, for loving our Chris and for being a woman of compassion and strength. I am cheering for you loudly as God uses you as a voice for those who need an advocate and a teacher. You are called ... anointed ... and appointed! Thank you for being such a patient and loving mom to the next generation of McLeod's ... Amelia Grace and Jack Burton.

Thank you, **Allie**, for loving Jordan and for believing in him. You are a gift from God to the entire family! I can't wait to see what God does in you and through you! Your devotion to the Kingdom of God is rare and compelling. I am honored to have you in our family. Thank you for being such an incredible fun, loving and compassionate mom to Ian Wesley.

Thank you, **Chris Barker**, for loving our Joy-Belle! What an answer to prayer you are! You are the young man for whom I have prayed for many, many years! You are a man of excellence and principle. Truly, you, my new son-in-law, are one in a million!! You are a man in whom there is no guile.

Thank you to all of the grandchildren who fill my soul with laughter and singing once again! From oldest to youngest ... **Olivia Mae, Ian Wesley, Wesley Eric, Amelia Grace, Roger Boyce, Elizabeth Joy** and **Jack Burton**. What a grand bunch of grands you are! You truly are God's opinion that the world should go on ... and on ... and on!

And now ... I must say ... to some very dear friends and sisters who serve in the Kingdom of God ...

Thank you, **Angela Storm**, for your gift of faith and of finance! Thank you for using your organizational skills for the Kingdom of God. But most of all ... thank you for YOU! Thank you for being one of my dearest friends. The fact that we get to work together is the icing on the cake of life!

Thank you, **Monica Orzechowski**, for being so generous in sharing your creativity and passion with the world. Thank you for your dedication, your vision and your integrity. Your heart is the most beautiful part of you! I am praying that God will accomplish what concerns you.

Thank you, **Kerri Cardinale**, for your voice, your friendship and your boldness! Whenever I think about you ... I know that God loves me!! What a gift you are! Keep singing your song, girl! Keep leading us to the throne room of grace!

Thank you, **Sue Hilchey**, for a lifetime of friendship, laughter, companionship and support. You are truly the most unselfish person I have ever met.

Thank you, **Terra Robinson**, for being such a great little sister in the faith and for loving Just Joy! Ministries! I so appreciate your servant's heart and your willingness to serve us all. You are loved and appreciated!!

Thank you, **Linda Zielinski**, for giving to us your expertise of administration and of mailings! What a gift you are to us! I admire you ... respect you ... and honor you!

Thank you, **Kim Pickard Dudley**, for your wisdom, your business acumen and your heart for young women. Thank you for your prayers, your friendship and your support!

Thank you, **Christy Christopher**, for going to battle with me time after time after time! You are a force to be reckoned with!! How I love our friendship!!

Thank you, **Barb Thrasher Finity**, for your labor of love among the saints! You have literally encouraged people around the world on behalf of Just Joy! Ministries! Thank you for your sweet notes of encouragement and your unconditional belief in me.

Thank you, **Shannon Maitre**, for being the little sister that I never had. By the way … I love you more. End of story. Period. #therewereneversuchdevotedsisters

Thank you, **Kim Schue, Lisa Keller, Lynn McNerney, Janie Sperrey, Carol Cervo, Debbie Bogdan** and **Lynn Glaser**, for serving days and weeks and months on end. Thank you for praying without ceasing, for serving without complaining and for loving beyond measure.

Thank you to **Debby Edwards, Dawn Frink, Marilyn Frebersyser, Kathy Pierce, Lynn Fields, Patricia Apy, Camella Binkley** and **Diane Phelps** … for being the best girlfriends that I could ever ask for! Thank you for wisdom, for meals, for support, for prayers, for late night phone calls, for creative thinking, for giggles, for shopping trips and for truly bringing me joy in all seasons of life!

And finally … let me say thank you to one more group of people … the professionals who have given to me wisdom and professionalism that is rare in the world today …

Thank you, **John Mason**, for believing in my message and in my ability to communicate it. You are a gift, my friend. You are a true masterpiece of God's own design!

Thank you, **Chris Busch**, for living with integrity and for quite simply being a man of honor in a world of compromise. When God made you … He threw out the mold! You are as close to perfect as they come!!

Thank you, **Scott** and **Julie Spiewak**, for helping promote the message and the books that God has given to me. I am praying for you as you pray for me.

Thank you, **Kim Worden**, for relentlessly working on my behalf. You are a delight with every word you speak, each e-mail that you send and every phone call that we share.

Thank you, **Suzi Wooldridge**, for being one of my new favorite people on the planet! I feel like we are kindred spirits! Thank you for believing in the message and publication of this book.

And finally ... and most importantly ... Thank You, Father! You are the song that I sing and the story that I tell. Thank You for using me in Your Kingdom, for your purposes and for Your glory! I love serving You with every breath that I breathe! Thank You for life ... for joy ... and for strength ... in every season of life!

Joy is With Him!

For many years, I was a depressed Christian. I loved the Lord dearly during those dark days and even knew that I was going to Heaven when I died. However, I was unable to discover the joy of His presence on earth. I felt removed from hope and peace. The black hole of depression was my constant companion and my ugly friend.

The depression that I experienced was birthed in a nearly six-year battle with infertility. I sent 5 babies to Heaven all of whom had only lived in my womb for between 12 and 20 weeks. Each conception was a miracle … and each interruption was a crashing and heart-breaking devastation.

My hormones were out of control … my hopes were dashed … and my arms were empty. And worst of all, my heart was broken.

Every morning when I got out of bed, the black hole called my name. That taunting black hole followed me around from the kitchen to the laundry room to the grocery store.

Although I already had given birth to 2 delightful, precocious, lively little boys … I knew that I had been created to be the mother of more. Motherhood was my destiny and my calling. Why was it all so difficult?

After losing 5 babies prematurely, I then became unable to conceive. My body was in full-blown betrayal and everything that a woman was supposed to do was impossible for me.

I spent years on high doses of fertility drugs and knew the despair of a cycle of disappointment every month on day 28 … or 29 … or 30.

During these sad, frighteningly hopeless days, I also developed an all-consuming addiction. The addiction of my own choosing was not found in over the counter drugs or in obsessive shopping. The addiction to which I tied myself did not come in a bottle filled with an alcoholic substance nor was it attached to binge eating.

My addiction ... my drug of choice ... was truly a miracle. While I was depressed and reeling from the pain of dashed hopes, unanswered prayers and a body that was betraying me, *I became addicted to the Word of God.*

During the days of blackness, the Bible became a source of joy and light.

During long nights of hopelessness, the Word of God spoke promises and purpose.

During months of discouragement, the Bible was a voice of encouragement and blessing.

My arms were still empty but my heart was full. My prayers were as yet unanswered but I was falling in love with Him ... over and over and over again.

I would go through every single dark day of depression to know Jesus the way I know Him now.

I would walk through the valley of infertility and disappointment all over again in order to be the defiantly joyful woman that I am today.

During that season of healing and restoration in my life, I asked the Lord to allow me to become an expert on joy. What a bold prayer for a barren woman to pray!

And now I eat joy ... share joy ... talk joy ... enjoy joy ... distribute joy ... splash joy ... know joy ... and have built a life on the joy of His presence.

In *"Joy For All Seasons!"*, I will be sharing with you the principles that I have learned from my addiction to the Bible. I want you to nestle down into the scriptures that have the word "joy" in them and I also want to share with you what the Lord taught me from each particular verse.

Perhaps you can view it as if you are receiving daily vitamins of the very best kind! I hope that you will swallow completely and enthusiastically this daily injection of joy and strength into your dark and disquieted soul!

I don't know what has caused your depression and discouragement, but I can assure you that His Word is able to heal you and encourage you. Believe me … I know from personal experience that His Word is a miraculous healing drug and a wise and faithful counselor.

Join me … as I share with you … my journey to joy!

"You make known to me the path of life; in Your presence is fullness of joy; in Your right hand there are pleasures forever."

— PSALM 16:11

The joy is found wherever He is.

He is in every sunrise and sunset.

His presence is visible in the first flowers of Spring and in the glorious leaves of Fall.

His voice is heard in the symphony of worship and in the giggle of a baby.

His presence resounds in the roar of the ocean waves and in the majesty of snow-capped mountains.

He is found gently caressing His own in the trauma of emergency rooms and in the aftermath of violent storms.

He is found comforting widows and brokenhearted parents.

He is there in the humdrum of daily life when the dishes are piled high, the laundry is mountainous, and the bills never end.

He is there in unending days of loneliness and in the piles of tissues by your bed.

He is with you ... and you with Him ... and He brings the gift of Heaven's joy!

When I am being overtaken by the deceit of my emotions, what I really need is more of Him. In order to cultivate the joy of Heaven's grandeur in my puny, ordinary life I need more of His presence and more time spent at His beautiful and nail-scarred feet.

When my joy begins to fade and is often replaced by loneliness or depression, I am gently reminded by the Holy Spirit, *"Carol ... if you are lacking joy ... guess who moved?"*

All the joy I will ever need this side of Heaven is found in hanging out with Him. It is found when I relentlessly choose more of Him and less of me; it is found when I understand the value of intimacy with the Lover of my soul.

If you need joy to be more practical than poetic, perhaps these suggestions will propel you toward the possibility of joy:

Choose a Scripture that has the word joy in it and memorize it.

Say it again and again and again.

Sing a favorite song from when you were a child in Sunday school.

Sing it again and again and again.

Whisper a prayer for someone other than yourself.

Whisper it again and again and again.

Read your Bible at least three days a week ... then four days a week ... then five days a week ... until you have made it part of the substance of your life.

Sing at the top of your lungs while you are driving.

Invite some people into your home to pray.

Joy is a heartfelt and strenuous discipline that only the desperate are brave enough to choose. I must choose His presence in spite of the world that roars around me.

For those who lack joy, perhaps part of the dilemma comes from looking for joy in all the wrong places. We mistakenly believe relationships will deliver joy, or that it is possible to purchase joy at the mall along with Gucci, Godiva, and Gap. We think we will find joy at Disney World or at Harvard.

Those pursuits, and many others, may leave you empty and lifeless, but the joy of His presence will fill you to overflowing and will give you the undeserved, miraculous gift of abundant life.

BIBLE READING

Psalm 16

JOYFUL THOUGHTS TO PONDER

If joy is, indeed, found in His presence, then why do so many believers struggle with staying in a place of joy?

Is joy an emotion?

Write out your definition of the word "joy".

_____

_____

_____

Journey To Joy

All of our lives are a journey … a journey *from* somewhere *to* somewhere.

Perhaps your life has been a journey away from abuse toward emotional and physical health.

Maybe your life's journey has encompassed education, travel, and scintillating relationships.

Did you start life as a victim in a dysfunctional family and now you are proud to say that you have built a victorious family of function and faith?

My life's journey has often lingered in the land of depression but I can confidently say, now, that joy is my home address!

JOY DEFINED

In fifth grade, my beloved teacher, Miss Sullivan, taught her curious class of eleven-year-olds, that in order to define a certain word, one should never use the word itself in the definition. The rule that Miss Sullivan taught all of her eager students is an accepted grammatical rule that most savvy writers and wordsmiths follow implicitly.

However, I have discovered, it is nearly impossible to define the word "joy" without using the word itself in the definition.

The Hebrew definition of the word *simchah* is: *"joy, mirth, gladness; the joy of God."*

The Greek definition of the word *chara*, is: *"joy, gladness; the cause of occasion of one's joy."*

Due to my frustration at being a grammar elitist and knowing that substance is lacking by using a word in its own definition, I decided to dig a bit deeper and to valiantly endeavor to discover the root definition of the word "joy".

"Joy wrought by the Holy Spirit" was a definition that resonated a bit stronger in my frustrated soul because at least it gave some credit to the Holy Spirit.

And then, at last, I came upon this definition from a Hebrew dictionary I found among my father's archaic library: *"the blessedness that the Lord enjoys around the throne of God Himself."*

Although this definition uses a derivative of joy in the word "enjoys", I found myself completely agreeing with this ancient meaning found among stacks of dusty, dog-eared books.

Joy is the atmosphere of Heaven. It is the air God the Father Himself breathes in every day of eternity. And because joy is Heaven's delivered gift to me while I walk on planet Earth, it is my delight and strength to experience the blessedness that God on His throne enjoys.

Wow ... put that in your heart and marinate in it!

Joy is God's gift to us as we snuggle into His presence and hunker down into all that He is and all that He gives.

YOU ARE CORDIALLY INVITED ...

Have you ever been invited to dinner at a dear friend or family member's home and then been forced to sit and watch hours of vacation and holiday videos? Well ... consider yourself invited over to dinner at my life because I, too, am going to force you to view my journey to joy!

> *"Do not be grieved [or depressed] for the joy of the Lord is your strength."*
>
> —NEHEMIAH 8:10

You have an enemy who desires that you would live in a constant state of debilitating, relentless depression and discouragement. This enemy is unable to change the fact that you are Heaven-bound and have been guaranteed eternal life. He can do absolutely nothing about your entrance into Heaven's gates. Since he can't touch eternal life, what he attempts to do is to ruin abundant life. Don't let him do it!

You have a God who wants to inject you with His joy because it is God's miraculous, perpetual joy that will deliver strength to your life this side of Heaven's glory.

The devil does not want you strong. This diabolical laughing stock of a shadow of absolute nothingness wants you to be the weakest version of yourself possible and so he goes about it in one singular way: the devil attempts to steal your joy.

The devil is not just after your marriage, your health, your finances, your children, or your relationships. What he is really after is your joy and the way that he tries to access your joy is through your marriage, your health, your finances, your children, and your relationships.

Do not let the devil have your joy that Jesus died for! Stand toe to toe ... nose to nose ... with the accuser of the brethren and have a stare down. Hang onto your joy and declare in his face,

"Devil, you weak, whining, immature caricature of all that is not holy, you will never ... not ever ... not in a million Sundays ... or in a thousand eternities, have my joy. One of us is going down and it ain't gonna be me!"

If you release any of your joy to the enemy it will turn you into a weak, whining, and ineffective Christian because the joy of the Lord is your strength. Other than your salvation, I believe that your joy is the most valuable commodity you have been given while walking the surface of planet earth and breathing in oxygen.

The powerful gift of joy is able to give you indomitable strength during your days of pain and trauma. If there is anything the devil hates more than a Christian ... it is a joyful Christian.

Hang onto your joy. Don't ever let go of your joy because joy is what will give you the strength to fight and to carry on every day of your life!

BIBLE READING

Nehemiah 8:9-12 and Psalm 5

JOYFUL THOUGHTS TO PONDER

How is it that joy gives strength to the life of a believer?

What are some things that you can do to "hang onto your joy"?

Make a list of some things in your life that are worth celebrating and then add to that list all of the ways that you can celebrate with joy!

_____

_____

_____

Your Heart's Desire

Everyone I know desires to live a joy-filled life.

Young moms and seasoned moms are desperate for it …

Teenage girls long for it …

Widows and widowers search fiercely to rediscover it …

Empty nesters, single women, corporate executives, divorcees, and college students all wonder where joy can be found.

The sad truth is that often depression and discouragement place themselves within easy grasp, don't they? Frustration and sadness are usually within whispering distance. No one needs a GPS to find the blahs, melancholy or hopelessness.

If we all long for it so intensely, where is it? Where is joy?

Depression and discouragement are known for their strong and paralyzing hold on men and women like you and me.

However, the miraculous discovery that I have found is that His presence is well able to demolish the chains of sadness and disappointment.

Will you continue with me on this amazing journey to joy?!

A BABY NAMED JOY

There were a group of shepherds who were defined by an inky and black existence. These men, who were the lowest dregs of society, spent night after hopeless night taking care of someone else's dumb sheep.

These uneducated men had no chance of promotion or pay raises.

The lives of these shepherds were defined by the most base and disgusting of components that were connected to the herd of beasts under their watch. The drool of sheep ... the disgusting dung of sheep ... and the perpetual sound of the "ba-a-a-ing" of sheep was all that these hopeless men knew. Day after day after unending day, sheep slobber adorned their robes, sheep dung clung to their toes and the cacophony of sheep filled their ears.

However, one night that began as the carbon copy of thousands of other dark, cold nights, the world of the shepherds was instantly invaded by the announcement of great joy! The heavens exploded in rare and glorious colors and the angels of eternity made a grand pronouncement into the hopeless world of the shepherds:

> *"And behold, I bring you good news of great joy which shall be to all people; for unto you is born this day in the city of David, a Savior, who is Christ the Lord."*

> —LUKE 2:10-11

The eternal reason the angels could announce that joy had invaded the atmosphere and culture of Earth was because joy had come in the person of a baby named Jesus. Heaven opened its portals that night and joy splashed into our lives forever. He came into our inky darkness and the joy of Heaven dripped into our world.

No matter how hopeless and dark your life seems to be, always remember that a Baby was born whom Heaven had named "joy". The life of this Baby changed everything for every person in all of history. His presence has come to earth and with Him He brought the joy of the atmosphere of Heaven!

A GARDEN OF JOY

I don't know much about agriculture but this is what I do know: when a farmer plants cucumber seeds ... cucumbers will grow. When a gardener plants sunflower seeds ... sunflowers grow in that place. It is true in every branch of agriculture and botany that you will always reap what you have sown. If you plant radish seeds, you will not be harvesting carrots. If you plant a rosebush ... there is no need to worry that turnips will grow in that place.

However, the Bible makes one exception to this valid and scientific rule:

"Those who sow in tears shall reap with joyful shouting"

—PSALM 126:5

If your life has held nothing but pain and sorrow and tears, let me assure you that your life holds more potential for true joy than the life of someone who has lived with a white picket fence guarding the tulips of their life. The Bible says all of your tears are going to miraculously reap a harvest of joy and rejoicing.

God takes the tears of disappointment and sadness, fertilizes them with His presence, and out of that place of deep pain will erupt an abundant harvest of joy. You are never immune to this miracle or left out of this promise.

Only God can take your worst defeat, your greatest pain, and your moment of raw sorrow and turn it into His miraculous and irreplaceable joy. Only God.

HERE HE COMES!

And now, if you are still struggling to find this solid by-product of His presence, let me just encourage you today to be grateful. Spend some time this very minute in heartfelt worship and thanksgiving and before too long the ripples of joy will begin.

When you begin to sing in spite of pain and disappointment, you will discover the most glorious gift of all ... He has arrived! He will come walking to you across the years of disappointment and gloom. He does not come alone but with Him comes the dynamic gift that follows Him wherever He goes ... the gift of joy!

BIBLE READING
Psalm 126 and Luke 2:1-20

JOYFUL THOUGHTS TO PONDER
What is your favorite hymn or worship song?

Why is it that the Bible promises "those who sow in tears will read with joyful shouting"? Have you found this to be true in your own life? Share an example.

If Jesus has been born in you, the world should see His joy in you. Make a list of the people in your life who need the gift of joy. Pray for them today.

_____

_____

_____

Just One Thing

What if I told you that there is one simple change that you could make in this year that would change your life exponentially?

Would you do it?

What if I told you that there is one daily discipline, which takes about 15 minutes a day, that is stronger than an anti-depressant, more powerful than a personal trainer, and brings greater comfort and wisdom than the most renown counselor you could possibly find?

Would you participate in this discipline? Would you?

What if I told you that I, a formerly depressed woman, currently experience such joy and peace in my soul that it reaches far beyond my circumstances, past the difficult people in my life and overcomes my socio-economic level?

What if? Would you believe me?

It is not a "magic" fix although it is indeed a miraculous prescription! I have found that participating in this simple yet meaningful practice delivers eternal rewards and rejuvenates the woman that I am with inexpressible joy and purpose.

Are you in? Are you willing to take the plunge with me at the beginning of this brand new year?

If you know me at all, and you understand the miracle that God has caused to happen in my life, then you know exactly what I am going to tell you to do.

Read your Bible.

Read your Bible every day with joy and delight!

Immerse yourself in its powerful principles and in its extravagant peace.

Think about the Word of God ... talk about the Bible ... make it part of your emotional DNA.

Read your Bible.

Did you know that the Bible has healing power over sin, sickness and emotional pain?

> *"He sent His word and healed them and delivered them from their destructions."*
>
> —PSALM 107:20

Did you know that the Bible is able to do for you what other resources are unable to accomplish in your life?

> *"My soul weeps because of grief; strengthen me according to Your word."*
>
> —PSALM 119:28

The Bible is the greatest source of healing, of comfort, of wisdom and of peace that has ever been known to humanity.

> *"This is my comfort in my affliction, that Your Word has revived me."*
>
> —PSALM 119:50

Whatever you have gone through in life, the Word of God has the power to heal and to assuage your pain! I guarantee it!

Whatever you will face in all of your tomorrows will be bearable because of the wisdom and strength found in the Word of God! I guarantee it!

So many people just simply don't know "where" to begin reading in the Bible. I don't believe in playing "Bible Roulette". Have you ever heard of "Bible Roulette"?! That familiar but frustrating game is when you just open your Bible and frantically look for a magic answer to whatever conundrum you have found yourself in on any given day of the year!

I believe that God's Word is powerful and a wise counselor. I also believe that the Bible holds the answers for God's children when applied appropriately, when treasured daily and when a heartfelt longing for God's opinion is desired.

If you are wondering how to approach reading the Word of God during this calendar year, let me give you a couple of suggestions:

1. Set aside 15 minutes a day to read your Bible. Perhaps on the weekend, you would be able to set aside 20-30 minutes a day. We spend our lives doing so many different and various activities and ignore the importance of daily time focused on God's heart and on God's will. God's heart and God's will is only found in the Bible ... it is His eternal gift to us!

   We go to the gym, play computer games, talk on the phone, watch pointless TV shows and clean things that will just need cleaning again tomorrow! The investment of time that you give to the Word of God will be the best investment of your entire life!

2. Choose a Scripture once a month to memorize. At the end of the year, you will be the beneficiary of 12 new Scriptures that are hidden in your heart! On the first day of every month, simply write out a verse on a 3 x 5 card and then carry it around with you. When you are waiting in a line, read your memory verse ... when you are in a doctor's office, read your memory verse ... when you are on the verge of frustration, read your memory verse. By the end of the month, it will be written on your heart!

3. When you are in a difficult situation in life, get on your knees with your Bible open. Ask God to speak to you through His Word. Reverently open your Bible and bask in all that He is and all that He has. The best place to start is to study the verses that are on your daily plan for that day.

4. Make it your personal goal to share with someone once a week what you are reading in your Bible. Ask God to open doors for you to share a Scripture with someone. Perhaps you could set a monthly appointment with a friend and determine that you will only talk about the Bible!

5. Remind yourself that as the children of God, we do not primarily read the Bible for information but for transformation. Even if your mind does not understand what you have read, your spirit is being renewed, strengthened and restored! I guarantee it!

"So I will keep Your law continually, forever and ever!"

—PSALM 119:44

BIBLE READING
Psalm 119:1-40

JOYFUL THOUGHTS TO PONDER
What is the best time of day for you to spend time reading your Bible?

Has God ever brought a Scripture to your mind when you were in a difficult place in life? What was that Scripture?

What Scripture verse will you memorize this month?

_____

_____

_____

Layers

I often feel that I live my life in layers.

Perhaps it is not that I actually live my life in layers ... but there are definitely layers that co-exist inside of me.

My external layer sometimes reflects what is going on inside of me ... and sometimes it doesn't.

I strongly believe in walking by faith and not by sight and often I am able to exude hope and joy on my face even when inner questions are causing indigestion of the soul.

Some people might call this being a fake ... or exhibiting a disingenuous persona. I prefer to acknowledge the fact that I don't believe that every disappointment should rear its ugly head and diminish the person I was made to be.

Not every pain has the right to take over my countenance or vilify my speech patterns. If I choose to mope my way through a glorious new day and verbally vomit on anyone who gets in my way ... that is giving pain and disappointment way too much power in my life.

I was made for joy.

I was made for hope.

I was made for faith.

I believe that it is the circumstances and the events of life that often deceive me into embracing attitudes and emotions that don't tell my true story.

My true story is that I have found a joy so pervasive and so amazing that nothing ... absolutely nothing ... is able to take it away.

Underneath that visible, external layer is the second layer of living that I deal with.

This second layer is the place where emotions or soul try to usurp authority. This is where the trouble begins. This is always where the trouble begins.

My soul often doesn't like what I am going through and so it whines and complains.

My emotions walk by sight and not by faith and so I continuously must rein them in.

This second layer is the two-year-old part of me. It is where the tantrums exist ... and where the selfishness reigns ... and where the right to be heard demands recognition.

But I am not sure that my soul is the best representation of me. I think that I was made for more than emotional spasms and for more than outbursts of bluster.

I am sure that when Jesus said, *"If anyone wishes to come after Me, he must deny himself, take up his cross and follow me,"* He was talking directly to me. He might have been looking at the disciples, but He was thinking about me.

"Carol, if you really want to follow me, you must die to self. You must die to your right to be heard. You must die to your right to be sad. You must die to your desire to let everyone know what you are going through."

The truth is this ... disciples of every generation are challenged to go to the deepest layer of self and discover that Christ is enough.

He is always enough.

He has always been enough.

He will always be enough.

The third layer of me is where I live by principle and not by preference.

The gut of me is where I know that I know that I know that He will never leave me or forsake me.

At the core of my being, I know that God is good and that He will always have the last word.

And so my third layer is actually the most genuine and truthful part of me.

The part of me that really matters has attached itself to a Truth so dynamic and powerful that nothing is able to move me from it.

My heart of stone has been removed and a soft heart of compassion and trust has taken its place.

I have experienced His presence where there is always fullness of joy.

I have been to the Rock and water has come pouring out for me.

I have shouted, "Grace! Grace!" to my mountain and it is about to move in Jesus' Name.

I no longer live in the darkness of emotional pain and disappointment but I gloriously walk in the light of His promises.

I have asked God the hardest questions that my human mind is able to conjure up and I have found Him to be enough. I have found Him to be more than enough.

The third layer must have the last word, the loudest word and the deciding word.

My countenance and my soul must recognize that they are not in control of the woman that I am. I am a woman whose identity lies deep within and who lives for Christ and not for self.

Oh ... I am well aware of the fact that my emotions and soul try to diminish the foundational principles in my inner being, however day by day I am learning that I am not a two-year-old any more.

I am a woman who was made for more than disappointment.

I was made for more than ranting and raving.

I was made for more than being "real" and sharing my side of the story.

I was made to share His side of the story.

From the cross of Calvary, Jesus looked across the millennia at my life, and said, "Carol, I am here, on this cross, so that you don't have to be. I am dying so that you can live abundantly. Carol ... I have taken not only all of your sins to the cross ... but I am also taking everything that will ever cause you emotional pain to the cross."

It's time for you to figure out your layers. What has the final say in your life?

Are you reacting to circumstances like a two-year-old? Or like the person that God created you to be?

Oh … I don't always get it right. But my heart's desire is to live to glorify Him and to keep my circumstances in their proper perspective.

The focus of my life is to rest in His grace and not in my emotional pain.

And so if you see me as only a girl with a smile on her face … a sparkle in her eyes … and a skip in her step … you will only be viewing that first layer … the visible part of me. However, if you take the time to look deep within my layers, my heart's desire is that you will see Him and not me.

BIBLE READING
John 3:22-36

JOYFUL THOUGHTS TO PONDER
Make a list of some of the "layers" that you have found in your life. Are these "layers" healthy or are they a distraction from abundant living?

Read John 3:29 & 30 again. How was John the Baptist's joy made full?

What are some habits in your life that need to "decrease" so that Jesus can "increase" in you? Spend some time praying over those issues today.

To Love and Be Loved

Valentine's Day ... some folks love it ... some folks tolerate it ... while others dread it!

Do you remember those Valentine Boxes we used to make in Elementary School? I remember carefully decorating those sweet boxes with shades of pink and red in the days leading up to February 14. I recall painstakingly printing my name in bold letters across the top of that important box and then deeply hoping for a Valentine from at least a few friends among my classmates.

As the years went by, I realized that Valentine's Day was not really about how many cheap cards were placed in a shoebox but in my ability to love and to be loved. When that realization took hold, the holiday known as "St. Valentine's Day" became a conundrum to me. I realized that February 14 would either embrace a greater and deeper significance or it would be frustratingly kicked to the corner of our heart.

Whether you are 16 or 86 ... here is my Valentine advice for you during this week that celebrates love and all that it entails:

If you are happily married ... wholeheartedly love your husband today. Live with no regrets. Love this man with reckless and complete abandon. Treat your husband in an extra special way on this day that was made to honor "love" and "romance". This need not cost a lot of money but it may require a lot of attention and heart. Fix his favorite meal for him ... watch his favorite movie with him ... find a copy of "your song" and play it for him first thing in the morning. Get up early and make coffee for him ... leave him a note on the dashboard of the car ... choose not to nag, criticize or complain for 24 entire hours!

If you are still waiting for your prince charming ... allow yourself to find fulfillment in the heart of the One Who knows you best and loves you the most. Even after you are married, Jesus should still be your First Love! It is so important for single women to "wait well" during these days of single living. While you are in the days or years of waiting, purpose in your heart to serve others and to become the best "you" that you can be.

Go on missions' trips!

Teach Sunday School!

Invite others over for dinner!

Baby-sit for free!

Prepare to run a marathon!

Take an extra class at college or at church!

Tell the pastor that you are available to serve your local church!

Women who "wait well" seldom "wait long" for fulfillment because they find satisfaction not in being loved but in loving others well!

If you have found yourself "suddenly single" due to rejection or divorce ... know that you serve a God Who will never leave you or forsake you. Do not build a wall around your broken heart but allow God to heal those broken places inside of you.

Pray with other single women and spend time with a mentor.

Join a Bible Study and allow your soul to flourish in the fertilization of the power of the Word of God.

Reject bitterness and embrace His power and His joy.

If you are a widow ... it's OK to enjoy a sweet memory or two ... but then choose to give to someone else today. Perhaps you could babysit for a young couple so they could go out to dinner. If you are not able to do that ... slip a young couple $10 or $20 so they can go out and enjoy the days they have been given to cultivate a lasting marriage.

I don't believe that celebrating love should merely be confined to Valentine's Day ... but we should love others well all of the other 364 days of the year! God has placed us here at this time in history to reveal His fruits to the world in which we live.

"But now, faith, hope and love abide, these three; but the greatest of these is love."

— I CORINTHIANS 13:13

BIBLE READING
I Corinthians 13

JOYFUL THOUGHTS TO PONDER
What are some of the attributes of Godly love?

Who in your life needs an extra dose of love this year? Make a point to love them well this week.

As you think about your life and days gone by, what one friend or family member has truly loved you in spite of your flaws and weaknesses? If that person is still living, write them a note or call them on the phone and thank them for their love for you. If this person is no longer alive, find someone who needs your love and spend time with them this week.

_____

_____

_____

In The Wait

Waiting. Who likes to wait?

Not this girl.

It seems like I have spent my entire life simply waiting for something … or for someone … or for God to move on my behalf!

How many ordinary days have dragged along when I had my heart and mind set on tomorrow?

Waiting. Tapping my toe. Checking my watch. Playing games on my phone.

Waiting in the doctor's office.

Waiting in the fast food line.

Waiting for my kids to call me.

Waiting for payday.

Waiting for answers to prayer.

Waiting for my destiny to unfold.

Waiting for Christmas.

Waiting for Summer.

Waiting to see my grandkids again.

Waiting.

The truth of the matter is this … we all have to wait for something! And it is my personal choice whether I will wait well or wait poorly!

I am a bit like Thomas Edison. Mr. Edison, after he failed more times than he succeeded, is famous for having said, *"I have not failed. I* have just discovered 10,000 ways that won't work."

So ... let me say ... in my best Thomas Edison imitation, "*I am not impatient. I have just discovered 10,000 ways how **NOT** to wait!*"

And in having discovered at least 10,000 ways how NOT to wait ... I have also discovered healthy ways in which to wait.

But wait a minute ... I am getting ahead of myself here. You are going to have to wait for the good stuff while I point out the troublesome behavior of someone (that would be me!) who hates to wait and who has exhibited the raw behavior of impatience time after time after time.

First of all, refuse to worry while you wait. Worrying is a waste of time, energy and emotions. Worrying does not solve anything for anyone. All worry does is sap vital energy that could actually be given to hopeful expectation. Worry is infamous for destroying a vast number of "todays".

I have had to convince myself time after time after time that the definition of prayer is not "worrying on my knees".

Don't do it. Don't worry while you wait.

Don't be negative while you wait. Don't conjure up every worst case scenario that could possibly happen in a moment of frustration. Don't gossip and criticize others. While you are waiting, throw away negativity like yesterday's garbage.

Don't do it. Don't be negative while you wait.

Don't waste your life while you wait. If you are waiting for a spouse, don't waste every Friday night with a box of tissues while watching a Chick Flick and eating chocolate ice cream. If you are waiting for babies to arrive, don't waste your days poring over baby name books or being jealous of your friends.

Don't do it. Don't waste another minute of your life in frustrating and childish behavior while you wait.

Don't become bitter while you wait. Don't mistakenly suppose that nothing will ever change for you. Bitterness always turns into selfish anger. Always. Anger will change a fruitful life into a futile life before you are able to tap your fingers or painstakingly yawn one more time.

Don't do it. Don't allow bitterness to become your middle name when you find yourself in the wait.

And finally, don't whine and complain while you wait. Don't allow impatience to come out of your mouth. No one wants your verbal vomit to show up in their otherwise delightful life and truly, no one is interested in your impatient germs. Quit coughing up your demanding agenda on your irritable schedule.

Don't do it. Refuse to allow the frustration of delay and postponement to come out of your mouth.

Trust me. I have discovered 10,000 ways how NOT to wait ... remember?!

So what should you do while you wait? *Now this, my friend, is the valuable stuff for which you have been waiting!*

You might consider investing yourself in some productive and healthy activities while you are waiting for your prayers to be answered and for God to move on your behalf. Volunteer at a homeless shelter. Babysit for free for a young family. Take an elderly couple out to lunch and ask them what they have learned about marriage. Go on Missions trips. Invite people into your home for dinner and a game night.

You can do it! You can serve others while you are waiting for your circumstances to change!

While you are waiting for your prayers to be answered, pray for someone else! The world does not revolve around you and your specific purpose or lack thereof. Make a list of others who need your prayers and then commit to praying for them every day. And while you're at it, let those people know that you are praying for them. Write notes of encouragement and send Scriptures to them.

You can do it! You can pray for others while you are waiting for your prayers to be answered!

Talk the language of hope! Every time you are tempted to whine or complain, stop yourself immediately and change your language to that of hope! Hope should be the native tongue of someone who is waiting. Learn to speak it just like you would learn to speak a new language before visiting a foreign country. The only language that should be spoken in the waiting room of life is the language of hope.

That's H. O. P. E.

You can do it! You can talk the language of hope because it is just more fun to believe!

And finally, worship your way through the wait! Sing yourself to sleep at night and whistle while you work. Hum while you pray and keep a symphony of genuine joy stirring while you are waiting for God to complete His work on your behalf. The song of your heart should be at its loudest when you find yourself in the waiting room. A seemingly endless wait should never silence the song of your life but should turn it up to resounding and echoing proportions.

The most powerful song is always heard right before the dawn of a new day!

> *"Wait for the Lord! Be strong and let your heart take courage! Yes, wait for the Lord!"*
>
> —PSALM 27:14

BIBLE READING

Psalm 27

JOYFUL THOUGHTS TO PONDER

In what way does "waiting" actually make you stronger?

What was one thing in your life that you waited well for? Is there anything that you waited poorly for?

What does it mean to "wait well"?

_____

_____

_____

Your Words

Your words.

Your words have the power to destroy or the power to encourage.

To build up or to tear down.

Your words can ease someone's pain or viciously magnify their regret.

Your words can plant a magnificent garden ready to blossom and spring forth in a glorious array … or your words can stir up weeds and discord in an otherwise beautiful life.

Your words.

Your words can stick the knife in and then twist it while gouging out someone's very heart … or your words can be a healing oil and a soothing ointment.

Your words can lovingly speak of truth with a kind tone, gentle verbiage and heartfelt compassion … or you can go ripping into someone's already raw emotions and cause traumatic and undeserved damage.

Your words.

In the center of your face, located halfway between your mind and your heart, is an opening called your "mouth". Inside that mouth is a muscle that weighs about one pound. This muscle is known as your "tongue".

Do you see where I am going with this?

Your tongue is located between your mind and your heart for a reason. Your mind and your heart have the massive power to control every word that this one pound tongue of muscle creates.

Your tongue may be the most powerful and influential muscle in your entire body ... but it is controlled by your thought life ... and by your emotional preferences.

Scarey, huh?

Maybe you don't fight the same battles that I have fought over the years with this one pound piece of overgrown, opinionated arrogance, but I have had to give myself some very strict guidelines concerning my tongue.

My tongue has placed me into more trouble than I dare relate ... it has shamed me and caused pain in the lives of the people who I know the best and love the most.

My tongue has not been pretty. My tongue often stinks. Bad breath of the very worst kind.

Halitosis of the heart.

My tongue has reared its ugly head in selfish, explosive language and I have wished too many times to count that I was able to push the re-wind button and erase something that I have spoken in emotion and in unbridled reaction.

Is anybody with me, here?! Or is your speaking record immaculately clean?!

"Guard your heart above all else for from it flow the issues of life."

—PROVERBS 4:23

My heart has been infected and reveals its dread disease through the words that I choose to speak.

My heart doesn't want to be guarded ... it wants to regurgitate its ugly self all over the people in my world.

Verbal vomit. Not a pretty picture, indeed.

The Bible doesn't say to express your heart ... it says to guard your heart. Control your heart. Give your heart some healthy boundaries.

And then ... if my heart weren't enough to deal with ... there is my mind. That over-thinking, analytical, anxious piece of human software.

My mind. My brain. My thought life. My. My. My.

After all ... if I think it ... then I have the right to say it, right?!! WRONG!!!

"For as a man thinks within himself so is he."

—PROVERBS 23:7

I don't know how this is possible but it is ... if I think it ... then I become it.

If I think angry, critical thoughts ... then I will become an angry, critical person.

If I think fearful, negative thoughts ... then I will become a fearful, negative person.

If I think ... then I will become.

I must not say everything that I think, feel and believe. I must not. I must discipline my tongue to download its soundtrack not from my heart or from my mind ... but from my spirit.

"Examine me, O Lord, and try me; test my mind and my heart."

—PSALM 26:2

I must ask God to clean out my heart and my mind. I must lay down my will on the examining table of the Great Physician and allow Him to do open heart surgery and a craniotomy on me.

You see ... my tongue is not my problem. My problem is the infection that lurks in my heart and the germs that have attached themselves to my mind.

Only the Great Physician is able to heal the disease that I have allowed to fester in the deepest parts of me.

And, as I am healed, I become more like Him. As I am healed, I begin to think like He thinks ... I begin to feel what He feels ... I begin to speak words that His tongue would speak.

You see, when the Great Physician is invited to treat my mental and emotional plague, He not only takes out the infection ... He makes me like Him.

What joy there is on the operating table of His presence and His power!

Your words.

Your words have the power to bring life and purpose back to a discouraged husband's beat-up heart.

Your words bring hope to your mother in her golden years.

Your words help your children dream big dreams and to slay huge giants.

Your words set the atmosphere for your home in a dynamic display of joy and peace.

Your words give loving direction to a friend who is floundering with self-esteem.

The words that you speak today are the seeds that will be harvested in your life tomorrow.

If you give loving words ... you will receive a bountiful harvest of love.

If you speak hopeful words ... you will be the beneficiary of the hope that is an anchor in the storms of life.

If you utter words of encouragement ... the encouragement you give to others will boomerang straight back into your heart.

If you declare words of faith and healing ... yours will be the mind and the heart that is miraculously healed.

Your words.

"Death and life are in the power of the tongue and those who love it will eat its fruit."

—PROVERBS 18:21

The words that you speak today determine the banquet from which you will eat tomorrow.

Your words cook up a recipe for your life that will be enjoyed for years to come.

Your words.

Speak well.

BIBLE READING

James 3

JOYFUL THOUGHTS TO PONDER

What is simply the nicest thing that anyone has ever said to you?

Why does the Bible teach, "Death and life are in the power of the tongue"?

The Bible doesn't say to "express" your heart ... it says to "guard" your heart. What is the difference between those two activities?

_____

_____

_____

Fear Not!

I had lunch with a friend this week and we were talking about the weather, and about wedding decorations and about her cute, lively puppy. As we shared lunch at a lovely restaurant, served by an attentive waiter, nibbling on salads and sipping cup after cup after cup of coffee, our conversation turned from talking about our kids to talking about our fears.

Crazy, huh?!

Fear.

Not the *"I'm afraid of the dark"* kind of fear ... or the *"Is there a monster under my bed?!"* kind of fear ... but Fear.

Actual fear.

Uncontrollable fear.

Can you relate? Are you afraid of anything?

The fear that my friend and I were talking about was the kind of fear that starts in the gut of your stomach and travels by rushing adrenaline to your heart and then manifests itself in a panic attack or worse.

We were discussing the ISIS kind of fear ... the failing economy kind of fear ... the culture is out of control kind of fear.

The big stuff. Fear with a capital "F".

Even as we were talking, I felt my mouth go dry and then that dismal, sobering feeling of despair rushed over my heart.

It was at that moment that I looked at my dear friend and said, *"This is when we need to stop listening to ourselves and start talking to ourselves."*

I started telling my sweet friend a story that had been seared into my memory from an experience that I had about 35 years ago.

Craig, at that time, was on staff at a church that was fixated on the end times. The pastor told us to store up food in our attics and to hoard water in our basements in order to prepare for "the end".

What?! I had just given birth to our first son and I couldn't imagine the world coming to an end while holding this gift of new life in my arms.

The fear that was simmering in my impressionable heart was enormous and I was teetering on the edge of depression.

Now, every Monday night, during this fearful and anxious time in my life, one of my single friends came over to our 1,000 square foot home and we watched *Little House on the Prairie* together while she got her baby fix from holding precious Matthew.

Do you remember the Ingalls' family? Pa … and Ma … Laura … Mary … Carrie … and their good old bulldog Jack?!

One autumn Monday evening, the TV story of the Ingalls' family was about a particularly difficult winter through which they were living. The snow was piled up past the windows of their log cabin, their food was scarce and the family wore coats, mittens and scarves even while inside the family home. Laura and Mary daily went out into the lean-to where Pa had placed the discarded cornstalks from their annual harvest. Laura and Mary twisted these cornstalks into small pieces of fuel for the family fire. The Ingalls' sisters' hands were bleeding from this daily chore and their little lips were chattering; but these girls would sing the hymns of the church while they twisted the cornstalks.

> *"Bringing in the sheaves, bringing in the sheaves,*
> *We shall come rejoicing bringing in the sheaves."*

Does anyone else remember this episode?

God spoke to me that evening while I watched this pioneer family television series with a bowl of popcorn in my lap.

> *"Carol … life has always been hard. Every generation has faced difficulties and challenges. But I have been faithful. I never leave my*

children. I will be with you and with your family no matter what the future holds."

Nearly four decades ago, God spoke to my fears through a wholesome story that had actually taken place over a century earlier.

But back to my lunch conversation this week ...

And so my friend and I while drinking coffee, stopped listening to ourselves and began talking to ourselves!

My dear friend and lunch companion shared with me a Scripture that God had given to her as she dealt with her out of control fears.

"See, I am sending an angel ahead of you to guard you along the way and to bring you to a place that I have prepared."

—EXODUS 23:20 NIV

Wow! We both looked at each other in amazement! God, the Creator of the Universe, the Father of Jesus and the Giver of the Holy Spirit, loves us so much that He sends angels to help us and to guard us along the difficult places in life!

Wow! Just Wow!

My friend and I realized in that moment that there was absolutely nothing to be afraid of! We serve a God Who is well able to take care of every generation, in every circumstance no matter the risks.

We also realized that our mistake had been in focusing on what was wrong with this world rather than staying focused on the immense power of an all-loving God.

My heart recalled the words of David, the Psalmist and the giant-killer:

"I have been young and now I am old, yet I have not seen the righteous forsaken or His descendants begging for bread."

—PSALM 37:25

What are your fears in life? Are you afraid of cancer ... of losing someone you love ... of poverty ... of who will be the next president?

Are you anxious over the balance in your checking account ... of rebellion in one of your dearly loved children ... or whether you will still have a job at the end of the month?

You need to stop listening to yourself and start talking to yourself!

You need to start focusing on the power of the God of angel armies and stop fixating on the fears that will probably never happen!

And in that place of being captivated by the Father and by Who He is, a sweet peace will rush over your heart just like it did for Lisa and I in the restaurant. You will find, like we did, that fear will disappear as you determine that no matter what your circumstances may look like, you will simply remember that He is faithful. Time after time after time.

And the next time you find yourself afraid, perhaps you would find that a powerful antidote to fear is to simply sing in the lean-to, just like Laura and Mary did.

> *"I know Who goes before me ... I know Who stands behind!*
> *The God of angel armies is always by my side!*
> *The One Who reigns forever ... He is a Friend of mine!*
> *The God of angel armies is always by my side!"*

BIBLE READING
Joshua 1:1-9

JOYFUL THOUGHTS TO PONDER
What were you afraid of as a child? What were you afraid of 10 years ago? What are you afraid of today?

How have your fears changed over the years?

Why did God tell Joshua, "Be strong and courageous!"? Why does God tell anyone to be strong and courageous?

_____

_____

_____

The Best Addiction

Addictions. We all have them.

Some addictions are healthy ... some are benign ... others are devastatingly harmful.

Let me explain.

I am addicted to unsweetened iced tea with a generous squeeze of fresh lemon in it. I imbibe this beverage every single day of the year ... Winter ... Summer ... Spring and Fall. The wind can be wailing ... the temperatures dropping ... and a multitude of snow particles can be in the forecast ... but I sit at my desk with a tall glass of lemon-graced unsweetened tea poured over cubes of ice. I do, indeed, drink more than one glass a day ... but who's counting?!

My addiction to unsweetened iced tea is benign ... it doesn't hurt me and it doesn't help me. It does, however, make me very happy.

I am not bold enough to reveal my harmful addictions, although if you think of things like sugar, carbs and butter ... you might be in the right area of addictive and harmful behaviors. The truth is ... I have never met a carb that I didn't like. 'Nuff said.

My friends will also tell you that I am addicted to college basketball, Christmas music, grandchildren, the beach and reading. I will let you discern which of those addictions belong in the healthy or benign categories!

Addictions. We all have them.

What drives us toward the things that we love? Who selects the things that we allow to take up a permanent place of residence in our hearts? Who determines what dominates the stuff of our daily existence?

Who decides whether a person loves shopping or hiking?

Biscuits or cucumbers?

Books or football games?

Solitude or the party life?

Are we pre-wired for these addictions or does life somehow program us for the things that we like and dislike?

All I know is this ... I didn't like professional football until I married Craig McLeod. As far as I was concerned, football was just a bunch of sweaty, muddy men chasing each other and a ball while grunting. And then, because I loved Craig, I began to love the things that he loved. BC (Before Craig), autumn Sunday afternoons were spent taking long walks among rustling leaves, enjoying rejuvenating naps with large doses of classical music thrown in. AC (After Craig), autumn Sunday afternoons became a time of raucous behavior in front the television while eating pizza, wings and ice cream. "If you can't beat 'em ... join 'em," became my wifely motto.

I didn't like college basketball until Matt and Chris were about 6 and 8 years old and the battle of Duke vs. UNC began in our home. I was hooked. March Madness has become a national holiday for us. I kid you not.

I wasn't much interested in anyone's grandchildren until I had some of my own. Now ... I can't get enough of other women's grandbaby stories and pictures. If you share yours with me ... I will probably laugh, cry and drool. I am addicted to grandchildren. Guilty as charged.

My healthiest addiction began when I was just a little girl hanging out with my dad in the early morning hours before dawn. I would meander down the stairs while the rest of the house was still snoring in their respective beds. Even the family cat was not awake yet to rub her white, furry softness against my little girl legs.

Dad would always be sitting at the kitchen table with a steaming cup of coffee, laced generously with milk, in his left hand. Open in front of him was his Bible and to the right of the Bible was a red pencil with which Dad underlined verses in his Bible. He also made notes, written in that same red pencil that always seemed to need sharpening, on those computer cards of the 1960's. I still have some of those computer cards to this day ... they are among my earthly treasures. I have them stashed away in my Bible.

When I snuggled up to Daddy with my long blonde hair all tangled and my wrinkled pajamas still on, he would begin to talk about the Bible to me.

He would tell me the stories of David ... and Abraham ... and Noah ... and Esther. He would quote to me some of his favorite Psalms and encourage me to learn those precious verses in the early morning darkness.

Dad would tell me the about Paul's missionary journeys and of the bravery of Peter. He would then write out a verse or two on a computer card and hand it to me so that I could memorize the verses that he had selected. It was a delight that Dad actually trusted me with the Word of God!

When the rest of the house began to stir, I would quietly slip away from the table and begin to get ready for the day. But a need in me had been filled ... I had spent time with my father and with my Father in the Word of God. I felt like the richest little girl in the world.

I am most proud of the addiction that I developed when in the company of my earthly father. I learned to love the Bible.

Although nearly half a century has passed since living in the same home with my dad, I still can't begin a day without valuable time spent in the Word of God.

There is an emptiness inside of me that the only the power found in the Bible is able to fill.

I feel that I have cheated myself, and the world in which I live, when I haven't spent time reading the Psalms or the Book of John or one of the Epistles on any given day of my life.

The addiction that I have to the Bible makes all other earthly addictions seem cheap and distracting. The mornings ... the minutes ... the days ... that I have spent with the Bible open in front of me have been the most fulfilling days of my life.

Nothing else satisfies my soul like time spent in His presence reading His love letter that was written just to me! Nothing!

Now ... I know that Jesus doesn't begrudge me my glass of iced tea ... nor does He frown upon the laughter that happens in our home during college basketball season ... and He even encourages me to spend time at the beach in the sunshine and sand that He created ... but there is something about a Father and His girl spending time together reading the Greatest Book ever written.

I come to Him just as I am ... sleepy, wrinkled and tangled. He looks at me with love in His eyes and calls me away from the temporary pleasures of this earth. He longs for me to invest my life in the things that will actually count for all of eternity. He knows that it is in the place of choosing Him and all that He is where I will at last discover fulfillment, purpose and rest.

Who needs carbs anyway?! I have Him!

"Turn your eyes upon Jesus,
Look full in His wonderful face.
And the things of earth will grow strangely dim,
In the light of His glory and grace."

BIBLE READING
Psalm 20

JOYFUL THOUGHTS TO PONDER
What are some of your unhealthy, yet benign, addictions in life?

What are some of your healthy addictions in life?

What is a favorite childhood memory that you have?

Life: Measured by Time

Life flies by, doesn't it?

Have you ever stopped for a moment and achingly wondered, *"Where has it all gone?"*

"Why ... I was a teenager just yesterday!"

"When did my children grow up?! Where did the fingerprints on the windows ... and the mountain of unfolded laundry ... and the car seats disappear to?"

"I was only married last month ... wasn't I?! How can my groom have gray hair and I, his bride, have wrinkles?"

"I am certainly not old enough to be a grandmother! I was just playing with dolls last week!"

Time. It roars by, breaking all barriers of sound and light, with apologies to no one.

Time is an avalanche that seems to gather speed as the years fly by in a blur of memories, heartache, happiness and challenges.

How can we grasp and hold onto this precious commodity called "time"? Why does life slip through our fingers like water through a sieve?

I remember my grandparents and parents talking about *"the good old days"* with a longing in their voices and a far-away look in their eyes.

I understand now.

I understand that the time and place known as "yesterday" can only be reached by traveling down the back and well-worn roadways of my heart.

The good old days ...

When my kids were little ...

When I was young ...

When my dad was still here ...

When more of life was in front of me rather than behind me ...

All of my beautiful "when's" have aged into a lovely basket of exquisite memories that are appropriately identified as "then".

So much of my life is now in the past tense and will never, ever happen again. How valuable are all of the yesterdays stored as cherished treasure in this woman's heart!

Slow down, time! Stop accelerating faster and faster and faster!

Life ... stop speeding out of control!

After six decades of living, I suppose that I have learned a thing or two about the passage of time and about the brevity of life, and about the intrinsic value of both.

One of the ingredients that indeed will reckon a life as glorious is that life on earth was never meant to last forever. A minute was never meant to be an hour ... an hour was never meant to be a day ... and a day was never meant to be a week.

A week was never meant to be a month ... a month was never meant to be a year ... and a year was never meant to equal a lifetime.

The glory of life is found in its sure and certain passing. Life is always moving at a rapid and purposeful speed, isn't it?

Nothing ever remains the same.

Nothing ever remains the same and that is what makes each moment a grand gift and causes each ordinary day to become a treasure of eternal value.

Life should never be measured by the perpetual ticking of minutes on a clock or by the constant passing of months on a calendar.

Life is more than the candles on my birthday cake ... the obvious wrinkles on my face ... and by the gray hairs that are multiplying on a daily basis.

Life should always be calibrated by the prayers I have prayed ... by the children I have embraced ... by the songs I have sung ... and by the people I have helped.

Life is the fulfilling culmination of books that I have read ... by the places that I have traveled ... by the leisurely walks that I have taken ... and by the hands that I have held.

One of the dearest lessons of wringing the absolute joy and wonder out of life is the ability to maintain a thankful heart through every season.

A lifestyle of thanksgiving has the miraculous power of turning trials into triumphs and morphing pain into purpose.

Learn to appreciate what you *have today* before time and regret cause you to appreciate what you *had yesterday.*

What you choose to do today is able to vastly improve the value and impact of all of your tomorrows.

Each day is too short for me to pray all the prayers that I long to pray ... to love all of the people that I care about ... to reach out to all of the ones who need a helping hand ... to read the books that I want to read ... and to sing the songs that were meant to be sung.

However, each new day is a rare and priceless opportunity to try it all again. And so at the onset of a fresh dawn I determine to pray ... to love ... to reach out ... to read ... and to sing.

And it is in that singular determination that I am able to build a life of breathtaking length and magnificent impact.

You know all those things you have always planned to do ... all of those great things that you have dreamed about accomplishing with your life? You should go and do them ... today if possible.

Tomorrow has not been promised to us ... and today is the greatest gift that has ever been given.

Your life will lengthen and stretch when you determine to enjoy the generous and gracious present that has been given this day.

The bounty of life is not found in the length thereof but it is always enthusiastically discovered in the moment.

And, after all, we were not really made for "time", were we? We are creatures of eternity and so this life is not all that defines us, fulfills us or renews us.

This time… this day… will evaporate like the dew on the morning grass. But the value of the vapor that defines the life we have been given is found in the priceless and unending stuff of which eternity is made.

> *"He has made everything appropriate in its time. He has also set eternity in their heart, yet so that man will not find out the work which God has done from the beginning even to the end."*

—ECCLESIASTES 3:11

BIBLE READING
Psalm 90

JOYFUL THOUGHTS TO PONDER
What has been your favorite season of life thus far?

What is God teaching you in your current season of life?

If you could give advice to the 18-year-old you, what would your advice be?

_____

_____

_____

Not My Will

We are about to celebrate the week known as "Holy Week". It is the achingly beautiful week that the Christian Church recognizes to mourn the death of Jesus and to celebrate His resurrection! It is a week of unbelievable betrayal, of loud hosannas, of good-bye meals and of desperate prayer.

This is a week that always sobers me and annually causes me to evaluate my faith. During this week every year, I walk up Calvary's mountain with Jesus and carry my cross beside Him. I want Easter to force me to examine the woman that I am and the course that He has for me.

Oh …I will celebrate on Sunday! I will shout with the crowds in triumphant procession but for today, allow me to evaluate who I am and who I am becoming in the story of Christ.

Jesus took the three disciples who had been with Him on the Mount of Transfiguration to the Garden of Gethsemane.

Peter, James and John were the three that Jesus fiercely desired to stand with Him in prayer. These were the three, Peter, James and John, who were closest to Him.

They had heard him laugh over the antics of children and had seen him cry at the tomb of Lazarus.

They had celebrated miracles with this Man Who went about only doing good.

They called Him their Teacher, their Friend and the Son of God. They knew Who He was … make no mistake about that.

But this night, in the Garden of Gethsemane, while Jesus prayed ... Peter, James and John slept.

While Jesus sweat great drops of blood ... the great triumverate snored.

While Jesus cried in agony ... the three friends, whom He trusted, slumbered.

Peter, James and John knew that Jesus was about to die the violent death of a criminal and yet they dozed and drooled. Where were their hearts of compassion? Were they faithful friends or forgetful acquaintances?

Three times Jesus came to the disciples ... and three times they were sleeping. They couldn't wipe the dirt from their eyes and thus nodded into sweet dreams while Jesus fought in agony over His destiny.

Jesus was about to be brutally murdered in order that Peter, James and John could live forever with Him. And yet they couldn't stay awake for Jesus. What kind of friendship is that?!

We become outraged at the seemingly careless actions of Peter, James and John and yet how often have I been caught giving into the twilight of lackadaisical behavior when Jesus calls my name?

"Carol ... could you spend time with Me?"

I watch television when there are prayers to be prayed.

"Carol ... could you read my Word to you?"

I read novels when there are people to be loved.

"Carol ... would you worship Me?"

I snore while my culture crumbles.

Just as the Savior needed Peter, James and John ... your Savior needs you. My Savior needs me. He has entrusted us with the power of prayer. He has entrusted us with the Great Commission. He has entrusted us with the Gospel.

In this Garden, Jesus prayed, "Not as I will ... but as You will."

Have you ever tried praying that prayer when your life was crumbling? Have you ever prayed, "Father, Your will be done", when faced with cruel circumstances?

If we learn nothing else from this particular event in the life of Jesus, we should learn to pray while others sleep and to desire the will of the Father above all else.

When Jesus finally roused the three from their slumber, they had a view in the moonlight of a mob coming up the western slope of the Mount of Olives. After the mob, led by Judas, seized Jesus, Peter stayed in the courtyard of the high priest. It was there that Peter denied Jesus three times.

I wonder if Peter would have denied Jesus if he had prayed rather than slept. I wonder how different my life would be if I would pray ... rather than sleep.

BIBLE READING
Matthew 26:20-46

JOYFUL THOUGHTS TO PONDER
What are some of the issues and activities that keep you from praying?

Why does the Savior need His present-day disciples to spend time in prayer?

Share about a prayer request that has been gloriously answered for you. Also share about a prayer request for which you are currently praying.

_____

_____

_____

Indeed!

It was the final week of Jesus on earth.

The Son who had been sent from the Father to save all of mankind from their sin was now on the last leg of His earthly journey. Jesus was about to complete what He had come to accomplish.

He had been born of a virgin.

He had healed the sick and had raised the dead.

He had calmed storms and had multiplied meals.

He had taught us how to pray.

He had laughed ... taught ... cried ... discipled ... and had dug the very fabric of His heavenly heart into the rich soil of humanity.

He had been a friend.

He taught us all how to believe.

Jesus went about doing good. Day after day. In every way possible.

He confronted sin and pride.

He also confronted injustice and religion.

He had gone to weddings and to funerals. He had accepted dinner invitations and had gone on boat trips with friends.

He threw money-changers out of the temple yet partied with tax-collectors.

And He loved. My! How that Man could love!!

He loved children and He loved prostitutes.

Jesus loved His band of brothers and He loved John the Baptist.

He loved lepers and short people and women with issues.

He loved the demon-possessed and starving widows.

He loved because He is Love. He knows of no other way to be.

But there was yet more for Jesus to do. His task on earth was not yet complete.

It was time for Jesus to die.

Jesus went into Jerusalem on the back of a borrowed donkey and the crowds went wild. They cheered and threw their cloaks in front of him.

They waved palm branches and danced along the way. It was a ticker-tape parade in first-century style.

On that day ... on the day that we now call "Palm Sunday" ... Jesus was the talk of the town and there was a parade thrown in His honor.

These crowds, however, were fickle crowds. On Sunday they cheered ... and on Friday they jeered.

On Thursday night, Jesus needed some time with the Father. He went to a garden to pray. He took with him his closest earthly friends. Peter, James and John were with him in the Garden of Gethsemane that night.

Jesus prayed and they fell asleep.

Jesus cried out to the Father and they snored.

Jesus sweat great drops of blood while they drooled.

Some friends, huh?

His band of brothers was nowhere to be found on Friday. Matthew tells us that they all ran away.

> "All of Jesus' followers left Him and ran away."
>
> —MATTHEW 26:56

I wonder if Matthew wrote those words slowly with tears running down his cheeks. I wonder if Matthew argued with the Holy Spirit if this one particular detail should be included or not.

You see, Matthew wasn't merely pointing his finger at others ... he was indicting himself. No one stayed.

Matthew didn't stay.

Although Judas had sold Jesus and Peter had denied Jesus, what Matthew knew was that no one in the entire group of 12 had stayed faithful to Jesus to the end.

"All of Jesus' followers left Him and ran away."

Betrayal. Denial.

The band of brothers had become a bunch of cowards. Yellow bellies. Chickens.

> *"If we are faithless, He remains faithful for He cannot deny Himself."*
>
> —II TIMOTHY 2:13

While everyone else ran and hid ... Jesus remained true to the Father's call and to His purpose.

Have you seen yourself in the Easter story yet? Do you cheer when others are in agreement but run and hide when the going gets rough?

Do you enter into worship on Sunday morning with the roaring crowd but then turn and walk away because you are disappointed with the way your life has turned out?

Do you intend to pray but fall asleep instead?

Those are the questions that we all must respond to during the week of Palm Sunday ... of the Last Supper ... of the Garden of Gethsemane ... and of the Cross of Calvary.

What was Jesus experiencing as He walked through His last week on earth?

His beautiful body was scourged and whipped. This was why He came.

A crown of thorns was forced upon His head. He came for this.

He was hung on a cross between two thieves. His purpose was being fulfilled.

His side was pierced. The prophets said it would be like this.

What was Jesus thinking about when He hung on Calvary's Cross?

Let me just submit to you today that I believe that Jesus was thinking about you and He was thinking about me.

You and I were what kept Him on that cross. You see ... He really could have called 10,000 angels to get Him down.

He really could have arranged a miracle and never felt the violent blast of a nail piercing His hands and feet.

The Man Who raised the dead, healed the sick,

   cleansed the lepers, forgave the prostitutes,

      multiplied food, calmed the storm,

         turned water into wine and set the captives free from demons ...

   ... that Man chose to stay on the cross.

That Man named Jesus chose to die.

The Roman government didn't murder Him.

The Jewish people didn't crucify Him.

Jesus chose to stay on the cross.

And while He was hanging there ... suspended between life and death ...

   between earth and Heaven ... between good and evil ...

   between light and darkness ... between His Father and Hell ...

That man was thinking about you and He was thinking about me.

We kept Him on the cross. Our sin put Him on the cross but His love for us kept Him there.

> *"But He was pierced through for our transgressions, He was crushed for our iniquities; the chastening for our well-being fell upon Him, and by His scourging we are healed."*
>
> —ISAIAH 53:5

When Jesus was coughing up blood ... you were on His mind.

When Jesus was engulfed in searing pain ... He was thinking

about you.

When Jesus was struggling for one last breath ... His dying thought was of you.

As His eyes were rolling back in His head ... He was picturing you.

> *"Therefore, since we have so great a cloud of witnesses surrounding us, let us also lay aside every encumbrance and the sin which so easily entangles us, and let us run with endurance the race that is set before us ...*
>
> *Fixing our eyes on Jesus, the author and perfecter of faith, who for the joy set before Him, endured the cross, despising the shame, and sat down at the right hand of the throne of God."*
>
> —HEBREWS 12:1 & 2

I have often wondered, *"Jesus, what was the joy that was set before You? What was the joy that you were focused on?"*

And the answer that He gave to me was so rich and so rare that it drove me to my knees, *"Carol ... you are my joy! I was focused on you!"*

You were the joy set before Him! I was the joy set before Him!

You were the reason that He stayed on the cross ... you were on His mind while He hung there ... and you are the reason that the tomb was empty!

Happy Easter, my friends! He is risen indeed!

BIBLE READING

Matthew 27:45-end; Matthew 28

JOYFUL THOUGHTS TO PONDER

What stone do you need the power of the Holy Spirit to roll away in your life? Ask your friends to pray with you today.

What did the angel say to the women in Matthew 28:5? What are you afraid of today? How does the resurrection of Jesus from the dead help you deal with your fear issues?

What is the command that Jesus speaks to His disciples in Matthew 28:18-20? How are you obeying this command in your life today?

_____

_____

_____

Embraced by Grace

Grace.

I have been thinking a lot about grace lately. Trying to wrap my mind … my heart … and my spirit around grace.

On one level it is such a religious word.

On another level it is an embrace of the very best and warmest kind.

I am intent on taking the religion out of "grace" and wrapping it around me like a quilt stitched with love.

Grace.

This is what I do know … God's grace is the very best gift that I have ever received.

I need grace. I am in desperate want of that which is offered to me so lavishly … so generously … so graciously.

Whatever blessing is yours today … you have it because of grace.

If you are reading this devotional today … you are reading it because of grace.

If you sing on the worship team … you didn't get there by yourself. Grace got you there.

If you have ever been on a missions trip … you didn't get there by yourself … grace got you there.

If you read your Bible this morning … you didn't do it or choose it by yourself. Grace did it for you.

If you want to know what grace is … read John 15:16.

"You did not choose Me but I chose you, and appointed you that you would go and bear fruit and that your fruit would remain, so that whatever you ask of the Father in My name He may give to you."

—JOHN 15:16

If you want to know what grace is ... memorize John 15:16.

Grace is what God gives to people ... flawed, broken and sinful people.

Grace is God's heart toward His dear children that results in the giving of all that He is and all that He has.

"The surpassing riches of His grace."

"The riches of His grace which He lavished on us."

"To the praise of the glory of His grace."

Phrases so beautiful that my heart literally aches with joy.

Grace is for me. I don't deserve it. I did nothing to earn it. And yet He gives it.

Imagine that!

You are valuable to God. Your minutes matter to Him. They matter very, very much.

God has been thinking about you since before the foundation of the world. He was planning for all of history past to roll out the red carpet for your life and for all that you would become.

But there was a problem. A big problem. A gargantuan problem.

There was a gap. An insurmountable, uncrossable gap.

Sin separated you from God ... but God wanted you back.

You are the crowning achievement of all that He created ... but sin and darkness had stolen you.

The cost was so great but God the Father was willing to pay it.

Did you know that the cost of an item is set by what someone is willing to pay for that item?

The Father was willing to pay anything ... anything at all ... to cross that uncrossable gap and to hold you in His arms once again.

God valued your life to such an extent that He knew that silver and gold were not enough to buy you back.

And so God ... the Creator of the universe ... the all-powerful, omniscient Being ... set the price for your life.

He bought you back with blood. He paid the debt in rich, dark red blood.

The blood didn't come from an animal.

The blood that was used as collateral didn't come from a dove ... or from a sheep ... or from a ram.

The blood that God the Father used in the greatest transaction of all eternity came from a Lamb. The only Lamb. The sacrificial Lamb.

God's Son. The Lamb.

That's grace.

Not only did grace buy you back ... but grace changed your past!

Are you ready for some great theology?! For some humbling truth?

> *"For all have sinned and fall short of the glory of God, being justified as a gift by His grace through the redemption which is in Christ Jesus; whom God displayed publicly as a complete sacrifice in His blood through faith. This was to demonstrate His righteousness, because in the forbearance of God He passed over the sins previously committed."*
>
> —ROMANS 3:23 – 25

WHAT?!!

Grace has passed over the sins that I have committed.

Just as if I had never sinned. My past is gone. Completely gone because of Jesus.

My sins are erased ... they are eternally gone. There is no more shame. No more paralysis. No more guilt.

There is only grace. Blood and grace.

I am undone!

"My sin – Oh the bliss! – of this glorious thought!

My sin, not the part, but the whole:

Was nailed to the cross and I bear it no more,

It is well! It is well with my soul!"

And the wonder of it all ... almost too beautiful to speak ... grace now treats us like we already are what we fear we would never become.

But there is a challenge to grace. A gut-wrenching, knee-shaking, head-dropping, dry-mouth challenge to grace ...

Because I have received grace ... I must give grace.

Because I have been the beneficiary ... I must benefit others.

Because of Jesus ... I must *be* Jesus to others.

I must cross that chasm of frustration, impatience, bitterness and anger ... and move towards sinful and difficult people with grace.

I must. There are no excuses.

Grace has removed all excuses.

If I have been given it ... I must offer it.

I must freely ... lavishly ... generously ... completely ... give grace.

I must treat others like they already are what I thought that they could never become.

And grace will enable me to do so.

The power of grace changes my past ... my present ... and my future.

The work of grace in me reaches out to you.

Grace. Too beautiful for words.

BIBLE READING

John 8:1-11

JOYFUL THOUGHTS TO PONDER

How did Jesus share grace with the woman caught in adultery?

What is your definition of the word "grace"?

Share about a time when grace was extended to you by a family member or friend. Share about a time when you extended grace to someone who wronged you.

_____

_____

_____

An Ache of the Soul

Do you have an ache inside of you today that is almost too much for you to endure?

Perhaps you are unable to actually pin the ache on any event or on any particular circumstance … but it is there nonetheless.

And it is tormenting you … a constant groaning of the soul.

Is there a painful emptiness in the gut of your being that perhaps has been caused by brokenness … by disappointment … or by rejection?

Are your sighs becoming epic in length and massive in sheer number?

Does every plodding day seem to fade away in the grayness of a foggy morning mist that even the sun is unable to penetrate?

Have you lost your will to sing … to dream … to hope … to move forward?

Perhaps you can relate painfully well to the words of the Psalmist,

> *"How long, O Lord? Will you forget me forever?*
> *How long will You hide Your face from me?*
> *How long shall I take counsel in my soul,*
> *Having sorrow in my heart all the day?*
> *How long will my enemy be exalted over me?"*
>
> —PSALM 13:1 & 2

There will always be times in life when the days are drab … when the

61

hours are meaningless ... and when the minutes are achingly mundane.

Not every day was designed to be the first day of Spring ... or a Fourth of July parade ... or a time of celebratory gift-giving.

Some days are March-like in length and in gloom. There actually might not be anything wrong ... but it seems like there is nothing much right, either.

Gray. Mundane. Aching. Malaise. Flavorless.

No sparkle. No music. No smile. No flowers.

In those moments of nagging doldrums and throbbing melancholy, I must embrace a strategy.

I must default to a strategy that brings hope ... that erases disquiet ... and that lessens emotional debility.

In the days of visceral fog and stark despair, I must pre-determine my default. It is essential that I stop listening to my soul and review, once again, the pre-planned determinate.

The Psalmist reminds me what this determinate should be ...

"But I have trusted in Your lovingkindness;

My heart shall rejoice in Your salvation.

I will sing to the Lord,

Because He has dealt bountifully with me."

—PSALM 13:5 & 6

And in this historic and beautiful psalm, we have found the plan. We have discovered a 4-step process that is so healing and so powerful that it has endured the test of time.

I have trusted!

When you don't understand ... try trusting.

When you are down in the dumps of life ... try trusting.

When you live in the pit of despair ... try trusting.

When your life has boiled down to absolutely nothing … try trusting!

Try putting all of your trust in a God Who is loving and kind. Stop listening to your emotions and then endeavor to live a life built upon the delight of trust and hope.

It matters not one bit how difficult or how disappointing your life has become because *the loving and kind God has not changed.*

He is perpetually good and He is eternally kind. Now … I can trust a God like that!

My heart shall rejoice!

You need to find your happy heart.

Talk to your heart and tell it what to do: *"Heart … it's time to rejoice!"*

The reason you can command your heart to rejoice is because your heart was never meant to rejoice in circumstances but it has always been called to rejoice in God.

Start singing an internal song even when you don't feel like it.

Let the song of your heart soar above the storm and above the fog.

There should be no disappointment bold enough to silence the song of your heart.

The song of your heart was given to you so that you could sing loudly and majestically … without pause and without whisper.

Your personal song is most clear and is at its resolute strongest when it is sung in the despair of human existence. Trust me. I know.

I will sing!

You know that song that was birthed in your heart and bubbled up in spite of your circumstances? Well … now it's time to open up your mouth and let that melody out for the entire world to hear!

You and God are the only ones who are able to enjoy the song of your heart … but the world will be dynamically changed and miraculously amazed by a believer who sings defiantly in the face of disappointment and despair.

Sing when you don't feel like it.

Sing when your soul is in pain.

Sing when the war is raging.

Sing anyway.

He has dealt bountifully with me!

What joy there is in that declaration! I serve a God Who has given to me beyond what I deserve!

I trust a God Who gives … and gives … and gives again!

My heart rejoices in His goodness and in His grace!

I *will* sing and I *will* honor Him!

So there, circumstances!

Take that, emotional fog!

In your face, discouragement!

And wait … what is that I hear? Do you hear it, too? I detect a sound echoing across eternity … it sounds like laughter!

Could it possibly be that when I choose Him … it brings joy to His heart?!

Could it be when I trust rather than panic … that it enriches His existence?

Could it be when I rejoice rather than weep … that He smiles?

Could it possibly be … when I sing in spite of personal pain … that He sings along?!

Could it be?!

BIBLE READING

Psalm 13

JOYFUL THOUGHTS TO PONDER

What does it mean to truly trust God?

Why do we, as humanity, have such a hard time completely trusting the Lord?

What is your favorite song to sing when your world is falling apart? Perhaps you should write out the lyrics of that song and ponder them today.

———————————————————————————————————

———————————————————————————————————

———————————————————————————————————

One In A Million

I am in a battle today and I have a feeling that some of you are, too.

Often ... I feel that I am in a battle with my destiny. With calling. With purpose.

Can you relate?

You know that you are "called" to something ... but perhaps you are not sure what that "calling" looks like.

You are well aware of the fact that God has made you for something extraordinary ... but your extraordinary seems lost in a gray haze of ordinary.

In the moments when facts battle with my faith for supremacy in my mind, I always go back to the basics. I try to remind myself why I am so passionate about what I have been assigned to accomplish during my 80 or so years on planet earth.

And these are the six things that it always boils down to for me:

1. I am called to make Hell smaller and Heaven bigger.

2. I have a God-given mandate to bring the joy of His presence to women who are snared in the inky blackness of depression.

3. I have been anointed to pray for women dealing with issues of infertility.

4. God has given me permission to share my addiction with other girls who are dealing with the troublesome and relentless issues of life. The addiction that I promote? Why ... it's to the Word of God, of course!

5. God has called me to raise up an army of women who are willing to pray even though all Hell is breaking loose … to worship while in the heat of the most ferocious battles of life … and to live by the principles found only in the Word of God.

6. God has charged me with the directive to teach the next generation of young women how to mother well.

Can you boil your life down to some basics? Can you verbalize, in about six sentences, why you are on the earth today?

Because … if you are unable to do so … life is going to rush by in a meaningless calendar of days that drain the very life out of you.

You were made on purpose … for purpose … and with purpose.

You are not a mistake or a number. I take that back … you ARE a number. You are one in a million.

No one has your genetic structure … your fingerprint … or your calling. No one.

I don't care whether you are the young and inexperienced 20-year-old, wet-behind-the-ears, innocent and raw puddle of intimidated humanity … or … you are the 80-year-old, washed up, wrinkled, overcooked and curmudgeonly grandmother.

You are made on purpose … for purpose … and with purpose.

Write down your purpose. Just six sentences will do. I dare you … write it down!

Don't waste another day in the frustration of not knowing who you are … or why you are.

And if words fail you … and you are unable to boil it down to six simple sentences … then just go and love somebody.

Pay for somebody's coffee.

Write a note to a childhood friend.

Make your husband's favorite meal.

Read a story to a child.

Invite a single mom and her kids over to dinner.

Take a widower out to dinner.

Call your mom.

Bring flowers home to your wife.

Don't make "purpose" harder than it actually is. You are here to make a difference in somebody's life every day of your life.

Love turns a simple life into a masterpiece.

Caring miraculously changes a meaningless existence into a symphony.

Don't get lost in the chatter of life but choose to love those you have been given without reserve and without regret.

Make a difference today. Make a difference every day.

It is why you are here. It is what will make your life meaningful and rife with significance.

If you want to live with passion … then forget about yourself … and look around you.

Who needs a helping hand?

Who needs an encouraging word?

Who needs a bouquet of love?

You got the job! You were created to fill up someone else's empty tank.

And while you are filling up others … you will find that you are being filled.

You will discover that giving … caring … loving … and filling others … are what it takes to build a life that is overflowing with joy.

The wonder of life is found when a simple human being decides to be a generous and extravagant giver.

So … if I could help you with your six basics … perhaps your list would look something like this:

1. Love
2. Give
3. Care
4. Bless
5. Encourage
6. Comfort

Now ... get to work!

And remember ... you are one in a million in the heart of God!

BIBLE READING

Psalm 139

JOYFUL THOUGHTS TO PONDER

Do you have 6 things that your life boils down to? What are your 6 things?

Why is it that in giving away to others that often we, ourselves, are filled up? Is this true or even possible?

What does this phrase mean to you, *"You were made on purpose ... for purpose ... and with purpose"*?

_____

_____

_____

The Pain of "Good-bye!"

Tell me ... how many times is it possible for one woman to say good-bye without having her heart irretrievably smashed into a million unmendable pieces?

How many times will I stand at the back door ... or in the driveway ... or at the airport ... with the tears of my heart uncontrollably splashing down my cheeks?

Saying good-bye to someone I love has to be one of the most painful components of this journey called "life".

I weep when I stand at the door and wave good-bye to my mom. Really?!! I am 60 years old and I still cry when I bid adieu to my mother!! Will I ever grow up?!

And don't even get me started on the absolute pain of leaving my children for long periods of time!

But since you asked ... I will tell.

It all began in August of 1999, when our oldest son, Matthew, drove away in his burgundy Jeep Grand Cherokee to begin his freshman year at a Christian university thousands of miles from home. His second hand vehicle, purchased by his generous grandparents, was packed to the roof with sheets, towels, pillows, a comforter, luggage, a waste paper basket, a laundry basket, books, pictures, and everything and anything else a young man of 18 years old could possibly need as he left his mom and his childhood home.

I stood at the door with both of his grandmothers, his 4 younger siblings and the family dog. I don't know who cried louder ... me ...

his 5 year old sister … his grandmothers … or the dog.

I remember thinking, "My number is up. Millions of women have done this over the course of history. Millions of women have let their children grow up and leave home. And now it is my turn. I hate taking my turn."

My very sensitive 10-year-old son piped up, "Well, Mom … at least you are not sending him off to war."

I cried louder.

Two years later Matt's younger brother, Christopher, left home for that same Christian university located thousands of miles away. The only difference was that Chris drove away in his silver Alero, which was also packed to the roof with stuff that I thought he needed. I stood at the door of the home that used to house a mom, a dad, 5 incredible kids and a dog. We were down to a mom, a dad, and 3 incredible kids. Even the family dog was no longer with us.

Where had the years gone? Why did the childhood years evaporate into thin air? How could these brilliant, talented, adorable kids that I had given birth to and then raised have the nerve to leave me?

One by one they left me …

Jordan, that little boy with the infectious giggle and never ending energy, left for college just before he turned 18. Where had 18 Summers … 18 birthdays … 18 Christmases gone?

Joy left 2 years later … the daughter who was named so aptly. She was the little girl who had danced her way into everyone's heart and filled our home with music. Her absence left a lingering fragrance in a nearly empty home.

And then … finally … the baby, Joni Rebecca, who had come to us later in life decided to attend that Christian university halfway across the country. There is no pain so real and raw as the pain of a mother saying good-bye to the last one.

Now what will I do?

Now who will I be?

Will there ever be anything as significant as being a mom?

Last week I stood at the airport and waved good-bye to Joni as she left to begin the second semester of her junior year in college. We both wept. When Joni turned to go into the airport, I gut-heaved. It wasn't pretty.

My heart was breaking with the pain of "good-bye" once again.

Why is this word, connected by the incongruous hyphen, so hideously agonizing for me?

"Good-bye" ... adieu ... farewell ... see ya' later, alligator ... auf wiedersehen ...

You can spell it one thousand different ways in a myriad of languages ... but I will never like its meaning. Never.

As a human, I want life to stay the same. As a mother, I want everyone to remain at approximately 10 years old and eat a nutritious, home cooked meal at my dinner table every night.

I want little girls to keep giggling ... little boys to keep teasing ... and birthday candles to stop multiplying.

But God has called us all to grow up and go.

We serve a God Who loves to see His baby birds flutter their as yet untried wings ... and then begin to soar into their destinies.

Although we serve a God Who never changes ... we serve a God Who loves to stir up change.

God's plan has always been a plan of birth ... growing into maturity ... changing with the seasons ... saying good-bye ... and beginning again.

We serve a God Who makes all things new.

We serve a God Who wants our security to be in Him and not in others.

We serve a God Who loves the family unit but Who does not want the members of that precious group of people to replace Him on the throne of our hearts.

And so God treasures and encourages each good-bye we are forced to say.

God gives to us people for a lifetime but He gives to us Himself for all of eternity.

God gives to us children for a season but He gives Himself in limitless relationship.

And so ... I blow my nose one last time ... stuff my tissue in my pocket ... and wipe the dripping mascara off my cheek.

I put the car in drive and force myself not to look in the rearview mirror.

It's time to begin again ... to pray for purpose ... and to discover the adventure of being 60 years old.

The empty nest is not nearly so empty when a weeping woman allows God to fill every corner of her heart.

BIBLE READING

Ecclesiastes 3

JOYFUL THOUGHTS TO PONDER

What is the most difficult "good-bye" that you have ever had to say?

What are some of the choices that have the capacity to take the "pain" out of good-bye?

What would your advice be to someone who is preparing to say a painful good-bye?

_____

_____

_____

For Moms Everywhere ... and For Those Who are Not Moms

Happy Mother's Day!

Whether you are an empty-nester ... a great-grandmother ... have 5 children at home ... or just found out that you are pregnant with your first ... you deserve to be celebrated with gusto!

This is the week that we salute moms!

Thank you, moms, for wiping noses ... for packing lunches ... and for figuring out 267 different ways to fix macaroni and cheese.

Thank you, mothers, for scratching backs and for doing laundry ... for dealing with play dough on the kitchen floor and with glitter on the living room carpet ... thank you for dying Easter Eggs and for baking birthday cakes.

Thank you, dear moms, for losing your girlish figure without complaint ... for understanding that stretch marks are a badge of honor ... and for memorizing "Pat the Bunny".

Thank you for staying up all night rocking a colicky baby ... getting up at the crack of dawn to potty train a strong-willed 2 year old ... packing a lunch for an independent 6 year old ... and then even brushing your teeth before you kiss your husband off to work.

Thank you, mothers everywhere, for saying an emphatic "NO!" to determined teenagers ... for sitting in the rain at soccer games, football games and t-ball games ... and for eating the crusts of PBJ sandwiches every day for lunch for decades.

Thank you for changing a diaper that no one else would change ... for reading "The Little Engine that Could" 147 times in just 48 hours ... and for peeling more potatoes in the course of your child's life than are grown in the entire state of Idaho.

You are a woman who regularly moves mountains ... you move mountains of laundry ... mountains of shoes ... mountains of toys ... and mountains of shoes. You are a mountain-moving woman!

You have willingly stopped carrying a make-up bag in favor of a 30-pound diaper bag.

You haven't worn perfume in years yet a particular fragrance lingers on your skin and on your clothes ... it is the odor of yesterday's apple juice and this morning's spit-up.

No one is able to adequately measure how much a single mother gives day after day after day but every mother knows that she has been given the greatest gift of all ... the gift of investing in the life of a child.

Motherhood, as wonderful as it is, is simply not the greatest goal for a Christian woman.

The greatest goal for any of us, either male or female, is becoming like Jesus.

If you have experienced the unexplainable miracle of motherhood, then the Holy Spirit will use your mothering experience to help you to die to self and to become more like Jesus.

If you are not a mom and will never be a mom, then the Holy Spirit, who is God's right-hand Man in working all things together for good, will use that experience to help you to die to self and to become more and more like Jesus.

If, like Hannah, you are crying out to God to give you babies, then the Holy Spirit will use these days of waiting as days of strengthening and will enable you to conform to the very image of the God Who created you.

From personal experience, 5 times over, I can tell you that motherhood is the most clarifying mirror that a woman ever faces in life. Motherhood has exposed to me all the ways that I am a sinner and not a saint.

Not being a mom has a way of revealing that, too.

Wanting to be a mom and having to wait for God to answer has a way of revealing our weaknesses as well.

You see, God uses both the presence and the absence of children in the lives of His dearly loved daughters as one of the primary tools that He uses to sculpture us into His beautiful image.

If you are longing to be called by the dearly loved term, "Mommy," and it hasn't happened yet for you, I can assure you that Jesus is enough to fill all of the empty places in you.

God loves you deeply and passionately whether or not you have children. Your Father desires to comfort you in your longings to raise children and He will strengthen you when you are overwhelmed by the never-ending demands of the children that you have created.

Unfulfilled desire is often the road that Jesus tenderly guides us on in order to give us something better. At the end of the road of waiting and of unsatisfied longings, He simply gives Himself. What could be better than that?

When we don't get our way and when something that we deeply desire eludes us, He gives to us, His disappointed children, a measure of His love that we would never know without the pangs of discouragement knocking at the door of our hearts.

So … let me start over by saying once again … *Happy Mother's Day!*

The second Sunday in May is not a day to remind women everywhere of their failures, their disappointments or who they used to be and look like … but it is a day to remind women in all walks of life the complete necessity of and the delightful fulfillment that is found in serving the Lord with gladness.

For all women … old and young … married and single … barren and fertile … this should be a day of promise and of purpose!

You, as a daughter of the Most High God, have the capacity to make a difference in the life of someone else! Your life counts for something beyond mascara, a number on a scale and the condition of your fingernails.

You, my sister, can make a difference in the lives of others and that is what it means to be a mother, anyway! Being a mom is no more and no less than the call to make an eternal difference in the life of someone younger than you are.

The plan of God for a woman was always to instill God-given destiny in the heart of a child. The child whom you serve can either have your DNA or not. It simply doesn't matter to God.

The plan of God for a woman has always been to love a child enough to fan the flame of dynamic creativity in the heart of that child. The child whom you love can either have your DNA or not. It simply doesn't matter to God.

The plan of God for a woman has always been to believe in a child unconditionally and to cheer them on enthusiastically until their dreams become reality. The child whom you believe in and cheer for can either have your DNA or not. It simply doesn't matter to God.

The plan of God for a woman has always been to pray for a child relentlessly until their hearts are filled with the power of God Himself. This child for whom you pray can either have your DNA or not. It simply doesn't matter to God.

To instill ... to love ... to believe ... to cheer ... to pray!

Any woman can do that for any child ... for any young person ... for any protégée ... for any disciple.

A mother, quite simply, is someone who believes when no one else believes ... who loves when all others walk away ... who prays when all others have given up.

Let me gently remind you that you don't have to be called "Mom" to be a mother. My prayer for you today, is that whether you are married or not ... whether you have birthed babies or not ... whether you have raised children or not ... you would invest in the lives of the next generation.

I pray that by your godly behavior ... by your words and by your actions ... by the way that you treat others ... that you will leave a legacy that shouts, *"One woman, who clings to Jesus, can make a difference that will leave ripples in the pool of eternity!"*

And from my heart to yours ... Happy Mother's Day!

BIBLE READING

I Samuel 1

JOYFUL THOUGHTS TO PONDER

Is Mother's Day a joyful holiday for you or a day of pain for you? Why?

Why might Mother's Day be a painful reminder to women? Is there anyone woman in your life that needs encouragement this year?

What is the highest call for a woman?

How can you mother the next generation although you may not have given birth to them?

A Four-Letter Word

Hope.

Just 4 letters.

H. O. P. E.

Where does it come from? Can it be bought or sold? How can just four letters make such a profound difference?

Can you smell hope? Does it bloom only in the Spring? Is there a store that sells hope ... a radio station that plays it?

What does hope sound like? Does it have taste?

Hope.

I have discovered that hope may be the most valuable intangible that I embrace. If I refuse to hope ... I am refusing to believe. I am ignoring an umbrella of faith.

I think that you can have hope without faith ... but you can't have faith without hope.

Life is hard, you know. Money runs out ... bodies betray health and youth ... people are difficult ... things need fixing.

Hope.

Is "hope" a Pollyanna-like attitude that ignores facts? I have never been very good at ignoring what I see or what I know. Perhaps I need to get over that.

I have found it much, much more difficult to live without hope than I have found it challenging to ignore facts. I will choose hope over facts any day. Every day, choosing hope seems like the best possible choice.

Can hope and facts co-exist? Are they compatible or mutually exclusive?

This is what I do know ... my facts don't tell the end of my story. What I see with my natural eye may actually be the pretense. What I am unable to see with my eyes may be the solid stuff of life.

And so I hope. I believe. I refuse discouragement and shake off despair. When my circumstances whine and scream and demand ... I choose the quiet whisper of hope.

When the facts of my life thunder and quake and pontificate ... I choose the sweet smile of hope.

We all choose. We choose hope or despair. Hope or discouragement. Hope or anything.

I don't know what circumstances are shrieking at you today but I can tell you that if you can choose to hope you are choosing strength. And joy. And purpose.

Perhaps the facts that we face are actually only the fog that surrounds and therefore clouds our view from the truth of hope. Maybe when the cloudiness of our human existence lifts, what we will realize is that hope was not ignorance but it was substance and held more truth that the fog. Perhaps what we will know then, that we don't know now, is that facts mask what is true, real and genuine.

And maybe, just maybe, what I need to remind myself every day is that hope is the foundation of the life that was meant for me.

And so I embrace a friendship with hope. I will wrap my mind around all that hope declares and promises. I will speak in hope and think about hope. I will use hope as the anchor of my very fragile soul.

"Be strong and let your heart take courage, all you who hope in the Lord."

— PSALM 31:24

BIBLE READING

Psalm 31

JOYFUL THOUGHTS TO PONDER

What are you hoping for today?

What is the opposite of hope?

How can you be an ambassador of hope to others?

What is a secret of staying in a place of hope?

_____

_____

_____

Discovering the Good Part

God is not finished with you yet. Regardless of how weary you are ... how old you are ... or what mistakes you have made ... God is not finished with you yet.

You may feel burned-out ... washed-up ... over-looked ... or under-paid ... but God has something for you that He has for no other person on the face of the universe.

His plan for your singular and ordinary life far surpasses anything that you have ever dreamed about ... asked for ... or imagined.

You might ask incredulously, "How can that be true?!!"

It is true because He is God and you are His beloved child.

It is true because you are the crowning achievement of creation.

It is true because you have the DNA of the Divine Himself stamped upon your humanity.

It is true because you are not here by mistake or by chance. You are here by His astounding creativity and by His focused plan. When you wonder if He has forgotten you, in actuality what you are doing is questioning and perhaps even doubting His love for you.

How can you question the God Who is defined with one eternal, perpetual attribute?

God is love.

Perhaps you could identify with the bossy Martha who felt the extreme need to confront Jesus about whether or not she was on His radar screen.

In Luke Chapter 10, Martha, crabby and discouraged, accused the Lord of not caring about her or about her specific frustrations. She called Him on it. (Not a good idea!)

These were the careless words that came out of Ms. Martha's overactive mouth when dealing with the false supposition that she was being overlooked by Jesus.

> *"But Martha, overly occupied and too busy, was cumbered (distracted) by the big dinner she was preparing. And she came to the Lord and said, "Do you not care that my sister has left me to do all the preparations alone? Tell her to help me."*

—LUKE 10:42

What "big dinner" has caused you to be overly occupied, too busy, cumbered and distracted?

What preoccupation has caused you to be frustrated with the Lord?

Have you been cocky enough... and mistaken enough... to accuse the Lord of not caring about you and your particular situation in life?

Have you been foolish enough, like the controlling Martha, to tell the Lord what to do?

I am guilty of it every single day of my too busy life! While I am preparing "big dinner" after "big dinner" after "big dinner", my priorities become confused and I take out my earthly grievances on my heavenly Lord.

Back off, Carol... back off. It's time to re-evaluate your priorities.

I have forgotten the power and the joy of time spent in His presence. I have overlooked the fact that disciples must sit at the feet of the Teacher.

And so I find myself at His feet once again. I discover, with Mary, the fulfillment that is found in only one place this side of Heaven.

I determine that my "big dinners" aren't worth the frustration.

Mary, the devoted, wise sister of Martha had chosen the good part... the very best part. Mary had her priorities straight.

> *"There is only one thing that is worth being concerned about, and Mary has chosen (discovered) the good part (that which is to her advantage) and it will not be taken away from her."*

—LUKE 10:42

I want to be a Mary while living in a Martha culture.

I want to choose like Mary chose, even when I am frustrated with my life.

I want to discover the importance of sitting at His feet when my world calls me to perform, to prepare and to produce.

I don't know what you are going through today but I can tell you this … the historical account of the totally opposite sisters is in the Bible for a reason.

Perhaps **you** are the reason that the Holy Spirit chose to include this very personal and embarrassing account in the Word of God.

You are not overlooked or ignored … He simply wants you to slow down, change your focus and choose the better part.

Martha blamed Mary for her frustration. Who are you blaming for yours?

The source of your frustration is not the other people that camp out under your fingernails … the source of your frustration is that you have not discovered the part of life that is to your advantage.

Focusing on self and your particular disappointments in life will never reveal your purpose.

You were made by God and for God and until you understand that, life will never make sense. Only in God do we discover our origin, our identity, our meaning, our purpose, our significance and our destiny. So linger today … linger at His feet.

Spend time in His loving presence and while you're at it … forget telling Him what to do. He's got it. He sees … He knows … and He cares.

When Love meets bossy … Love wins.

When Wisdom meets controlling … Wisdom wins.

When Kindness meets frustrated … Kindness wins.

Jesus is waiting for you to choose what truly matters in life … time spent at His feet. It's to your advantage.

BIBLE READING

Luke 10:38-42 and Philippians 4:4-8

JOYFUL THOUGHTS TO PONDER

What are the issues in life that frustrate you?

What does the Bible mean when it says, "Mary chose the good part"? What is the "good part" that Jesus calls you to choose today?

What are some of the daily activities that call you away from time spent at His feet?

Philippians 4:6-8 is a daily prescription to battle anxiety. On a 3 x 5 card, write out the steps that this passage promises will battle anxious thoughts. Share it with someone who is battling worry or anxiety.

Disappointment... Your Finest Hour

Are you disappointed today?

Have you ever been disappointed?

If you are older than 5 years old, you know exactly what disappointment feels like.

It is that gut level feeling of just being sad ... and at times sick over what might have been ... what could have been ... what **should** have been.

Disappointment is such a difficult emotion to process. Unfortunately, disappointment, this particular regret of the soul, has the capacity to take a person to his or her knees in the hopeless place of "if only" ... a place where hearts can be permanently paralyzed.

Where dreams are dashed.

Where goals are paused.

Where destiny is changed.

Or is it? Does disappointment actually have the power to change one's destiny? I think not.

> *"And not only this, we exult in our tribulations knowing that tribulation brings about perseverance, and perseverance, proven character, and proven character, hope. And hope does not disappoint because the love of God has been poured out in our hearts through the Holy Spirit Who was given to us."*
>
> —ROMANS 5:3-5

Hope does not disappoint.

Some of life's holiest moments are experienced during times of unwanted and undeserved disappointment. God loves to meet sobbing, wandering children in the valley of setbacks and in the wilderness of discouragement.

He lives for the moment when you come running back to Him because life has let you down again.

When you feel that your life has fallen apart... He meets you there. He is lovingly putting the pieces of your life back together.

When you mistakenly believe that you have been defeated one too many times ... He is there. He is perpetually cheering you on.

Truly, if you ever hope to experience victory again in your life, you will go to Him because victory only happens through Him. In Him. Because of Him.

So what does one do when dealing with the pain of disappointment? What is the panacea for those achingly bitter moments in life?

Disappointment is able to produce a work of grace and power when handled with humility and hope.

Disappointment can be your finest hour when you place your well-laid plans at the foot of the cross and humbly ask Him for His appointment.

When your heart is a mangled mess... hope has the power to heal.

When you are nauseous with regret and heartache ... trust gives life meaning again.

> *"And we know that all things work together for the good to those who love Him and are the called according to His purpose."*
>
> —ROMANS 8:28

Do you want to know what I believe? I believe that Romans 8:28 means exactly what it says it means.

We serve a God so powerful and so wonderful that He is able to knit together the mangled mess of our hearts into something breathtakingly beautiful.

When we concentrate on simply and passionately loving Him ... He is working behind the scenes of our lives to take every disappointment we encounter and work it to our advantage.

Although your heart may be hollow with the pain of aborted dreams and one downfall after another, hold on to hope.

Fan the flame of love for your Savior.

Trust in Him and in His goodness when your circumstances are bleak and discouraging.

Hope. Love. Trust.

Rather than remaining in a place of penetrating disappointment, know that because of the power and love of God, nothing this side of Heaven has the capacity to "dis"-appoint you.

Nothing this side of Heaven has the capacity to "dis"-appoint you.

You have been eternally and unflinchingly appointed for His purposes and His plans.

His appointment for your life trumps circumstantial "dis"-appointments.

Even if you were the cause of the disappointment ... you are not "dis"-appointed.

God has appointed you for favor, for blessing and for goodness in spite of you and because of Him.

"We exult in our tribulations ... knowing that ... hope does not disappoint."

So when dealing with the frustrating pain of circumstances gone awry, what does one do?

"We exult ..."

That word "exult", that the Holy Spirit and Paul strategically chose to use in this verse, means *"to glory in whether with reason or without."*

Rather than weep and wrap yourself in the flimsy comforter of discouragement, glory in your disappointment whether you can find a reason to do so or not.

You can glory in disappointment because God is still on the throne of your life. He is still in control. You have not escaped His love. And ... you are not "dis"-appointed.

He's got this. He's got you.

I am praying for you today, disappointed friend. I am praying that you will wrap yourself in the sure comforter of hope and then find a reason to glory in Him.

And if you can't find a reason to glory in Him ... do it anyway.

I am praying that you will experience His goodness in refreshing and extravagant ways.

I am praying that never again will you give someone or something the power to disappoint you. Your appointment remains sure and certain.

And, if my human voice has any comforting power, may I just remind you of some of the most restorative words ever penned by humanity:

"O soul, are you weary and troubled?

No light in the darkness you see.

There's light for a look at the Savior,

And life more abundant and free!

Turn your eyes upon Jesus!

Look full in His wonderful face.

And the things of earth will grow strangely dim,

In the light of His glory and grace.

His Word shall not fail you – He promised;

Believe Him, and all will be well.

Then go to a world that is dying,

His perfect salvation to tell!

Turn your eyes upon Jesus.

Look full in His wonderful face.

And the things of earth will grow strangely dim,

In the light of His glory and grace."

—HELEN LEMMEL—1922

BIBLE READING

Romans 5:1-5 and Romans 8:28-39

JOYFUL THOUGHTS TO PONDER

Is it humanly possible to "exult" in tribulations?

What is the most difficult thing that has ever happened to you? Were you able to worship your way through it?

How can disappointment be your finest hour?

_____

_____

_____

Trust His Heart

What moves you? What fills your heart with the echoes of eternity?

For me, it has always been words and melodies.

I remember as a little girl, hearing "The Christmas Song" performed on "The King Family Christmas Special" and it made my heart ache. I was probably only 7 or 8 years old that December and it was the first time that the beauty of lyrics and melody made me long for more. The voices of a 40-member family of 4 generations blended in deep and rich harmonies that made the tears roll down my little girl cheeks. I knew in that moment that some things are just so beautiful that they hurt. They hurt your heart.

About 20 years ago, I heard a song in a church cantata that moved me with the same type of deep and eternal beauty. I remember that it was when I was in a daily battle with depression and most days my soul was a hollow vacuum of nothingness. I went to church the Sunday before Christmas and was content to sit near the back, even though my husband was the pastor.

The cantata was cheesy at best and most of the music was woefully off pitch and embarrassing. The sheer inadequacy of the performance only added to my depression. Then, the choir director turned around and faced the audience. I felt like she was looking right at me. She lifted the microphone to her lips, opened her mouth, closed her eyes and sang in a rich contralto that echoed through the empty caverns of my heart.

> *"God is too wise to be mistaken*
> *God is too good to be unkind*

So when you don't understand,

When you don't see His plan,

When you can't trace His hand,

Trust His heart."

—BABBIE MASON

God spoke to me and I was never the same again. He spoke through the lyrics and melody of a song written by one of His dear children.

These words have become more than lyrics to me ... they have become solid theology. They have become a dynamic and powerful prayer. They have become a reminder in the darkest moments of my life that I can trust a God Who is good and wise.

"God is too wise to be mistaken ..."

My soul rests in the assurance that God really is too wise to be mistaken. God is never wrong ... not one time. I never know better than He does ... never. His wisdom never contradicts His Word ... and I rest there ... in that safe place of trusting an all-wise God.

God's wisdom never changes because God never changes. His mind and His heart toward His children thousands of years ago is still His mind and HIs heart toward His children today. If the ache of your heart is to know the wisdom of God, then you must read and agree with His Word.

If you read His Word and then question it or doubt it, then you really don't believe that God is too wise to be mistaken. When my mind and my circumstances tempt me to question the wisdom of God, I am brought back to a place of trust by the lyrics of the life of David, the psalmist and the giant-killer,

"And those who know Your Name, will put their trust in You, for You, O Lord, have not forsaken those who seek You."

—PSALM 9:10

God's wisdom is backed up by God's power. If He were only wise, with no power with which to move, than His wisdom would have a lesser effect upon our human lives. But because not only is He the God of all wisdom, but also He is the God of supreme and eternal power, I know that His hand always moves with the wisdom of His Name.

"God is too good to be unkind ..."

When I read those words, I weep. My heart melts within me at the goodness of the God who I love and serve. There is no unkindness in God. Everything that comes into my life is filtered through the wisdom, power and goodness of God.

Anything that God is, He is eternally. God is eternally and infinitely good. There is not one atom or cell of cruelty, unkindness or badness in God. God has never had a bad thought about you or has ever been tempted to be mean to you.

He is infinitely and lavishly good.

He is powerfully loving and wisely kind.

"So when you don't understand, when you can't see His plan ..."

How many times has THAT happened in your life?!

You don't understand what God is doing ... you can't see His fingerprint in the daily-ness of your day ... you don't hear His voice or see the handwriting on the wall.

You scream out for understanding and He is silent.

You demand an explanation from Heaven's heart and get nothing.

You wonder whether He is in control or not ...

What do you do at that lonely moment? Is there a place for your aching soul to be comforted?

"When you can't trace His hand ... trust His heart."

This is what you do at that confusing, lonely moment when you wonder where He is ... you trust.

You trust His heart.

You trust His wisdom and His power.

You trust His goodness that is never unkind.

You trust that He is enough to carry you through.

You trust the same God who David trusted.

You kneel before your Maker ... open your Bible ... and you trust.

BIBLE READING

Psalm 9

JOYFUL THOUGHTS TO PONDER

Where does trust begin for you? In your mind or in your emotions?

What does it mean to trust God completely?

Write out 10 adjectives that describe who God is.

_____

_____

_____

The Treasure of Today

I have been known to be guilty of longingly believing, like Scarlett O'Hara, that tomorrow will be better. I am often convictable of gazing yearningly into the glory of the future unknown and then mistakenly dreaming about fictional days that will most certainly be exponentially more wonderful than any real today could ever be.

I am sure that I will make more money next year ...

I am certain that I will lose at least 30 pounds in some magical month in my perfect and self-disciplined future yet to be lived ...

My marriage will be better tomorrow ... my house will stay cleaner next week ... I will solve all of my problems in this year ... and I will get to live at the beach very, very soon.

> *"Do not boast about tomorrow for you do not know what a day may bring forth."*
>
> — PROVERBS 27:1

But the simple truth is this ... today is the very best day of my life. There is no richer or fuller gift than the undeserved endowment of the present. Today is the moment of miracles ... the present holds the certainty of great wealth and the assuredness of an existence that is quite simply, too good to be true!

What is without fiction or exaggeration is that I am able to choose how much splendor I will wring out of today. Will I slog through uncommon moments and look dull-eyed at all that I have been given? Or will I embrace the ordinary miracles that rear their lovely heads in every waking moment?

If my focus is fixed on the remote possibilities of tomorrow, I will never be captivated by the wonder of now!

"... And tomorrow will be like today, only more so ..."

—ISAIAH 56:12B

If you are a mom, don't wish your child's life away by saying things like:

"I can't wait till my baby sleeps through the night ... or is potty-trained ... or learns to talk ... or goes to pre-school."

Indulge in the amazement of parenting that belongs to you today. When you are up with a colicky baby, pray that this little heart will stay soft toward the Lord and that he or she will walk in their God-directed destiny in life! Don't waste time mourning over lost sleep but celebrate the quiet moments of prayer that are so vital to the person that this little life will become.

Treasure every season, every day and every unscripted opportunity to pour love, time and training into the child who will become the legacy that you leave behind.

"In the day of prosperity be happy, but in the day of adversity consider – God has made the one as well as the other so that man will not discover anything that will be after him."

—ECCLESIASTES 7:14

It's not only mothers who deal with the propensity of believing the fantasy that tomorrow holds the treasure that today lacks. It's all of us in every season of life who agree with the falsehood that Scarlet so aptly stated, "Home ... I'll go home! And I will think of a way to get Rhett back. After all ... tomorrow is another day!"

What Scarlett was ignoring, and what you and I ignore as well, is that the choices we make today determine the joy and love we will experience tomorrow. The investment of whole-hearted engagement in the present will assuredly bring a wealth of resources tomorrow. However, the focus must be on living well today.

"My mouth is filled with Your praise and with Your glory all day long!"

—PSALM 71:8

Perhaps you would like to spend just a few minutes of today making some declarations with me that have the power to unlock the beauty and glory of all of the "now" moments of your life:

Today I will splendidly and extravagantly spend time listening to others and not merely thinking about me.

Today I will celebrate my current season of life and not foolishly long for different days, experiences and activities than the ones that have been delivered to my doorstep on this day.

Today I will not worry about what I do not have but will gratefully share all that I do have with the people I meet along the way.

Today I will use my fine china for no reason at all!

Today I will sing without regret and say "thank you!" loudly and often!

Today I will smile at children ... give words of encouragement to strangers ... and respond to the love I have been given.

Today I will wrap myself in the glory of creation ... whether it is in the sparkling and quiet white of a winter afternoon or in the firefly and watermelon moments of Summer. I will deeply inhale the luscious days of new birth that only Spring delivers and thoroughly appreciate the color and harvest of an autumn afternoon. Whatever season I am in ... that season will be my favorite!

Today I will be the very best "me" I can be and I will cease creating the fantasy "me" of the future.

I will make myself at home in the pleasure of today and find the fingerprint of God in every moment. I will listen for His heartbeat and for the song of life that comes only from Heaven.

I will tie myself to the present ... and be captivated by the gift of today!

"And my tongue shall declare Your righteousness and Your praise all day long."

—PSALM 35:28

BIBLE READING

Psalm 118

JOYFUL THOUGHTS TO PONDER

What are the three most important things that you can chose to do any day of your life?

How can you wring the joy out of an ordinary day?

What can you do to turn bad day into a good day?

Where do you often discover the fingerprint of God in your life?

_____

_____

_____

A Powerful Addiction

When I was living during the very darkest days of my life, I developed an addiction.

I was in the throes of depression due to years of infertility and repeated miscarriages. I sent 5 babies to Heaven when they had grown to between 12 and 20 weeks in utero. It was a time of non-stop grief, dashed hopes and raging emotions.

In addition to being heartbroken over my circumstances, having empty arms month after month and being in the throes of a dark and violent depression, I developed an addiction.

The addiction that I developed was not to over the counter drugs … it was not to alcohol … it was not to shopping or to chocolate or to binge-eating.

The addiction that I developed was to the Word of God. During those days, when the black hole of depression was calling my name across the cavern of grief, the Bible also was in hot pursuit of my soul. Before my circumstances ever changed, the healing power found only in the Word of God healed my profound and relentless depression.

What the Bible did for me … it can do for you.

How the Bible healed me … it can heal you.

The power in the Bible isn't only for me … it is also for you.

And so, today, nearly 3 decades removed from those days of ragged hormones and hopeless infertility, I want to share with you five ways that the Bible can change your life. I know … because it changed mine.

First of all, the Bible will help you stay focused on what is good.

It reminds you that our God is well able to take every situation and circumstance in our lives and use it for our highest good and for His greatest glory.

> *"And we know that all things work together for good to those who love God, to those who are the called according to His purpose."*
>
> —ROMANS 8:28

Secondly, the Bible will help you deal with temptations and your sin issues. I can tell you this … all of us are tempted to give in to sin. There is not a man or a woman alive who does not face temptation on a daily basis. When the Bible is your guidebook through life, you are able to develop a strength that will enable you to overcome.

> *"How does a young man* (woman) *keep his* (or her) *way pure? By keeping it according to Your Word."*
>
> —PSALM 119:9

The third way that the Bible can change you is to help you love the difficult people in your life!! If you are in constant frustration due to the irregular people in your life, know that God is not surprised by their presence. He may have strategically placed them in your life because He wants them to see Jesus in you!

> *"Love is patient, love is kind and is not jealous; love does not brag and is not arrogant, love does not act unbecomingly; it does not seek its own, is not provoked, does not take into account a wrong suffered."*
>
> —1 CORINTHIANS 13: 4 & 5

If you are wondering why you were born and what your purpose in life is, let me assure you that the Bible will definitely help you find your purpose in life! If you have found yourself wallowing in various choices, in lack of direction and in a purposelessness existence, ask God to give you His direction from the Word!

> *"For I know the plans that I have for you, declares the Lord. Plans for welfare and not for calamity, to give you a future and a hope."*
>
> —JEREMIAH 29:11

And finally, the fifth reason why you should be addicted to the Word of God is because it will help you focus on the important issues of life. As human beings, we often magnify the wrong things and minimize the important stuff. And so, when we are committed to the wisdom in the Word of God, our priorities are changed and we are able to focus on the eternal things of life this side of Heaven.

> *"When I consider Your heavens, the work of Your fingers, the moon and the stars, which You have ordained; What is man that You take thought of him and the son of man that you care for him?"*
>
> —PSALM 8:3 & 4

And so today ... for these 5 reasons and for thousands of other reasons ... read your Bible. Develop an addiction to the Word of God. I can guarantee you that you will become the person you were made to be when you delight in His Word!

BIBLE READING
Psalm 119:21-48

JOYFUL THOUGHTS TO PONDER
Make a list of the reasons why you should read your Bible every day.

What is the best time of day for you to read your Bible?

Write out your favorite Bible verse on a 3x5 card and ask God to give you the opportunity to share it with someone this week.

_____

_____

_____

I Will!

Have you ever wondered, *"Where do I go from here?"*

Has there ever been a moment when you have taken stark inventory of the personal investment in the life that you have been given and asked, *"What should I do with the rest of my life?"*

Or perhaps, in light of the truth that one's life passes with sonic speed, have you ever questioned, *"What will I do with the time that I have left on earth?"*

When I consider those unanswerable yet meaningful questions, I come up with a myriad of answers.

I know that I will continue to breathe in and out … to make my bed every day … and to figure out what to fix for dinner on any given night of the week.

But life is more than that. Life is more than recipes … and clean sheets … and gasping for air.

I know that I will continue to take long walks … to love the sunshine of Summer … and to delight in a good read.

But life is more than my preferences … my delight … and the things that I personally enjoy.

I know that I will play the piano … enjoy the comfort of a blazing fire in the winter … and anxiously await Spring's first bloom.

But life was never meant to be lived inwardly.

Life is more than me. Life is more than my pleasure … my comfort … and my ideas.

Life was intrinsically meant to be lived … richly and fully!

Life was designed to be experienced … with gusto and enthusiasm.

Life was always meant to be filled with eternal meaning.

Life, when lived appropriately and in its fullness, was meant to be given away.

As I ponder the next three or so decades of my life, I know that the years that I have remaining this side of Heaven will fly by. I am fully cognizant that each day is a miraculous gift and not to be wasted.

And so, I have made a few simple but important determinants.

This is how I will live with delight:

I will smile at children and kiss the irresistible faces of babies.

I will.

I will listen to the wisdom of those who are older than I and honor their perspective birthed from experience.

I will.

I will laugh every day … hug my husband … and call my mom.

I will.

I will stay in touch with old friends … make new friends … and try to send thank you notes.

I will.

I will celebrate Christmas with reverence and with enthusiasm.

I will.

I will embrace Thanksgiving as a lifestyle and not as a mere holiday.

I will.

I will wring the joy out of an ordinary day.

I will.

And, I have determined that I will live my life with immaculate honor and uncompromising morals. This is what I determine:

I will live with honor and with integrity every day of my life.

I will.

I will encourage others with my words and with my actions.

I will.

I will forgive quickly and will release my anger with the setting of the sun.

I will.

I will bring peace to relationships and to confusing circumstances.

I will.

I will choose to give more than I receive and to build a life on generosity not on material gain.

I will.

I will abstain from gossip and from partaking in negative conversations.

I will.

I will love truth more than ego.

I will.

But the greatest determinant of my life has always been, and will always be, to give my life away for the sake of the Gospel.

I will live to make Hell smaller and Heaven bigger.

I will.

I will spend time in the Word of God and ask God for revelation knowledge so that I can communicate the truth found only in the Word.

I will.

I will devote my life to prayer.

I will.

I will live personally and professionally by the moral principles found in the Bible.

I will.

I will allow God to use my life as a receptacle for His glory and for His goodness.

I will.

I will worship when the world is falling down around me.

I will.

I will decrease so that He will increase in me.

I surely will.

BIBLE READING

John 3:30 and Matthew 5:1-16

JOYFUL THOUGHTS TO PONDER

Write out at least 10 things that you can incorporate into your daily life. Entitle this list, "I Will!"

What does the word "delight" mean to you? How can you add "delight" to your life when you are going through a difficult time?

Write a thank you note to someone today who has changed you or brought delight into your life.

_____

_____

_____

The God of the "Hard"

Is anyone out there doing "hard" today?

Have formidable circumstances and troublesome events become a perpetual avalanche of disappointment?

You might feel as if you are at the end of yourself ... at the end of your courage ... at the end of your strength ... at the end of your joy. Perhaps your heart is not sure that it can gasp one more breath to get through one more day.

Is anyone out there dealing with the stress of difficult people? You know who I am talking about ... those misfits who are like fingernails on the chalkboard of life. It seems that every difficult person in the universe knows your cell phone number and uses it. Often.

Is anyone out there living in a rut? Just day after day after day of the same old ... same old. No highs ... no lows ... just the mediocre existence of the common man or woman. Ordinary. Average. Mundane. Boring.

Is anyone out there struggling because there is more of life behind you than in front of you? And ... you are seriously not sure that your life has ever meant anything to anyone. "Regret" is your new middle name and even the hope of something better is elusive and flat.

Where is God in the hard ... in the stress ... in the rut ... and in the regret? Does He even care that our lives are just so abysmally small and demanding?

I have a feeling that the words that God spoke to Moses nearly 3,500 years ago might resonate in your heart today amidst the hard ...

the stress … the rut … and the regret.

> *"The Lord said, 'I have surely seen the affliction of My people who are in Egypt, and have given heed to their cry because of their taskmasters, for I am aware of their sufferings. So I have come down to deliver them from the power of the Egyptians and to bring them up from that land to a good and spacious land, to a land flowing with milk and honey.'"*
>
> —EXODUS 3:7 & 8A

God had a message 3,500 years ago for Moses from a burning bush and He has a message for you today from a burning blog.

> *I have surely seen …*
> *I have given heed …*
> *I am aware …*
> *I have come down to bring them up!*

Are those words from the Bible stirring something within you yet? God is speaking to you who are dealing with hard … with stress … with the rut … with regret.

> *I have surely seen!*
> *I have given heed to your cry!*
> *I am aware of your sufferings!*
> *I have come down to bring you up!*

Never assume for one minute that God is ignoring your life or is unaware of your personal pain. ***God has surely seen!*** He is not blind nor is He oblivious. He is intently looking at your life and has not left you to flounder alone. ***God has surely seen!***

God has heard your prayer and help is on the way! God never ignores the prayer of one of His own. A fervent prayer cried … or whispered … or shouted … or uttered … or even thought … by a desperate child gets the attention of the Father. ***He has given heed to your cry!***

God is aware of your sufferings. All of them. He knows every detail of every disappointment of every pain-filled day and of every long, lonely night. There is nothing that you could tell Him that is "new" news to Him. He is acquainted with every hard situation ... every difficult person ... every average minute ... and every hopeless regret. How wonderful to serve a God Who understands human pain! *He is aware!*

And best of all ... *He has come down to bring you up!* God gets involved in the messy of our lives, rolls up His sleeves and gets to work. He will never allow one of His beloved children to remain needlessly in the swamp of perpetual pain or meaningless existence. *He has come down to bring you up!*

Scripture is not just a beautifully told, historically accurate story. The power of Scripture happens when it is applied to each of our lives in a practical way. I believe that when God spoke to Moses that day in the wilderness that He was speaking to you and to me.

God knew that we would all have times of "hard". Moses was in the wilderness because he had killed a man and was a fugitive from the law. Talk about hard!

God also knew that we would all have times of stress. Moses had no sheep of his own but had to be a baby-sitter for the herds of his father-in-law. Then ... God expected him to go talk to Pharaoh who actually wanted to kill Moses! I don't think that your difficult people are murderers. Talk about stress!

God knew that we would all have seasons of ordinary. Moses had been in the wilderness dealing with sheep drool and looking at the behinds of wooly livestock for 40 years. That's 14,600 days. That's 350,400 hours. That's 21,024,000 minutes. But who's counting? It's hard to measure mundane.

God knew that we would all deal with regret and the vacuum of a hopeless existence. Moses was raised in the palace to be the next king of Egypt but he had a problem with anger and then killed a man. Is there any hope for an 80-year-old man with a criminal record? Regret is the greatest exterminator of destiny known to mankind.

I have surely seen!

I have given heed to your cry!

I am aware of your sufferings!

I have come down to bring you up!

The God of Moses is the God of YOU! How about meeting God in the wilderness of divine appointment and listening to His voice in a burning blog? I have a feeling that I AM will say the same thing to you that He said to Moses ...

I have surely seen!

I have given heed to your cry!

I am aware of your sufferings!

I have come down to bring you up!

BIBLE READING

Exodus 3:1-16

JOYFUL THOUGHTS TO PONDER

What is the hardest experience that you have ever gone through in life? How did you see God's hand move on your behalf during that time?

Do you have a life experience that you regret? What did you learn from that experience? How is it possible to move forward from a time of regret?

Moses was called by God to lead the Israelites out of Egypt. What has God called you to do?

_____

_____

_____

In the Wait

What do you do when you find yourself in the wait?

We have all been there ... in the wait.

Waiting for God to answer.

Waiting for mountains to move.

Waiting for provision.

Waiting for healing.

Waiting for breakthrough.

Waiting for the storm to pass.

Waiting for someone ... anyone ... to notice that you are in the wait.

Some people seem to get breakthrough so easily ... for me it has not been like that. I have spent years in the wait.

Years waiting for God to answer.

Years waiting for God to move.

Years waiting for provision.

Years waiting for healing.

Years waiting for breakthrough.

Years waiting for the storm to pass. Who knew storms could last so long?!

Years waiting for someone to join me in the wait. Who knew the wait was such a lonely place?

Years in the wait. Years.

"Do you not know? Have you not heard? The Everlasting God, the Lord, the Creator of the ends of the earth does not become weary or tired. His understanding is inscrutable."

—ISAIAH 41:28

Sometimes I wonder if staying in the wait is more a place of power and less a place of weakness than I perceive it to be.

The days ... years ... that I spend in the wait are the times that I find myself spending volumes of time on my knees and days on my face in His presence. This powerful position makes the wait bearable.

The days ... years ... that I am in the wait, I spend more time in the Word. The Word comforts my weary heart while I am in the wait.

The days ... years ... that I am in the wait, I spend more time in worship. Worship takes my eyes off of what I don't have ... and Who He is! What power!!

It is in the wait that I discover I am not alone. He is with me in the wait. There is nobody I would rather wait with than Him. There is no one I would rather hang out with than Him. There is no one. Just Him.

He never gets frustrated with me ... or with the wait. That humbles me. I want to be like Him. I don't want to be frustrated in the wait ... or with Him.

The time spent in the wait turns my attention away from stuff and things and toward Him.

I find it a far more powerful choice to simply wait with Him than to wait for His hand to move.

It's in the wait that my life is joined to eternity's focus, to Heaven's power and to His perpetual and unconditional love. I become like Him and all that He is when I am with Him in the wait! I am able to access all that He has for me when I spend time in the wait with Him!

It is in the wait that I am changed. Revolutionized. Transformed. It is in the wait that I discover a strength I never before had. It is impossible to wait and remain weak when one waits with Him.

We all surely know that, if nothing else, one needs strength to wait. And the strength that is so desperately needed due to the wait is found in the companionship of Him Who is strong.

If you wait alone ... what frustration ensues!

If you wait alone ... what weakness prevails!

If you wait alone ... how slowly time passes!

But when you wait with Him ... what miracles happen!

"He gives strength to the weary, and to him who lacks might He increases power."

—ISAIAH 41:29

Waiting is not for wimps. But then again ... maybe waiting IS for wimps. Perhaps it is in the wait that wimps become warriors.

Have you ever noticed that in the wait ... temptation strikes with a ferocity unheard of in other places and in other situations?!

Have you ever noticed in the wait ... that you are tempted to say things that you shouldn't even think, much less have the audacious bravado to say?!

Have you ever noticed that in the wait ... the temptation to compromise beliefs and to forget about the promises of God is at a dangerously high level?!

It is Who you wait with that makes all of the difference.

If you are forced to wait ... wait with Him.

It is also ... in the wait with Him ... that I discover a tenacity that I never before possessed.

It is also ... in the wait with Him ... that I discover the purpose for which I have been born.

It is also ... in the wait with Him ... that vision is refined and that desires are purified.

I need the wait. I need to wait with Him. I need the work that happens in me during the wait.

"Though youths grow weary and tired, and vigorous young men stumble badly ..."

—ISAIAH 40:30

I think that I am only waiting … just hanging around until life happens … but He sees the wait as the stuff of which life is made. God made me for the wait and for the work that it accomplishes in me.

God designed the wait to be the place where treasure is discovered in my life.

The wait. It's the place where I become the person He desires.

The wait. It's the place where the pressure reveals the value.

The wait. Him and me. Me and Him. It's my favorite place.

> *"Yet those who wait for the Lord will gain new strength; they will mount up with wings like eagles, they will run and not get tired, they will walk and not become weary."*

—ISAIAH 40:31

BIBLE READING

Isaiah 40:28-31 and Galatians 6:7-10

JOYFUL THOUGHTS TO PONDER

What are you waiting for right now? How can you "wait well"?

How does the spiritual discipline of waiting serve to strengthen God's children?

What does it mean to "wait poorly"?

_____

_____

_____

Just 18 Summers

Summer lasts for exactly 95 calendar days. The Farmer's Almanac cites its onset as June 21 and lists its farewell on September 23.

95 days.

After 3 too-short months of mosquito bites and baseball games, the beach towels will be packed away ... the flip flops will be thrown away ... and the lazy, hazy days of Summer become a sweaty memory.

95 days.

And, do you want to know what else is a sobering reality of Summer? You only are given 18 Summers of 95 days each to share with your children.

18 chances to make sunshine memories and popsicle promises.

18 opportunities to read the books of childhood to your little ones ... to splash in the sprinkler ... and to make s'mores after a dinner of hot dogs and corn on the cob.

18 occasions to spit out watermelon seeds in the front yard ... to play kick-ball all afternoon ... and to catch fireflies in the waning daylight.

18 shots at teaching your kids to ride their bikes with no hands ... to play hopscotch on the front sidewalk ... and to make homemade ice cream before bedtime.

95 sunshine filled days fly by.

18 Summers evaporate into adulthood.

Rather than live with a heart-filled with regret when September 23 rolls around, perhaps this is the Summer you will endeavor to wring the pure sunshine out of every day. Here are just a few of my favorite Summertime activities that will last long after Autumn has come knocking at your door and well beyond the brevity of 18 Summers.

1. *Make a measuring stick at least 6 feet tall and about 6 inches wide. Mark off the inches and the feet on it so it resembles a huge ruler. Hang this piece of wood on a wall in your home and measure your children every year on June 21 and on September 23. See how much they have grown during the 95 days of Summer!*

    In addition to June 21 and September 23, choose other days of the calendar year to measure each child's height. Perhaps measure each one on Christmas day as well as on their birthdays. Put each child's name and the date next to the marks on your family's unique measuring stick!

2. *Go to the library at least once a month during the 95 days of Summer and choose books to read together as a family. Make it a celebration to read the books out loud to your children that were read to you when you were a child. It has been my experience that my daughters loved hearing "Tom Sawyer", "Mr. Mulligan and His Steam Shovel", and "Mr. Popper's Penguins" as much as my sons did! And, my three sons were riveted, as much as the girls were, by the adventures of "Caddie Woodlawn", "The Little House in the Big Woods" series and "Pippi Longstocking"!*

    Set aside time every day to read out loud to your children whether they are 4 years old or 14 years old. Pop some popcorn, hand out a bowl of fresh strawberries and put on classical music while you read.

3. *Have a contest at least once a week! Have you ever had a watermelon seed spitting contest?*

    Or a sidewalk chalk art contest?

    Or a whistling on a piece of grass contest?

    Or a cannon-ball contest at the neighborhood swimming pool?

    Or a decorate your bike contest?

    Or who can kick the ball the farthest contest?

Or who can hit the baseball the farthest contest?

Or a squirt-gun contest in the back yard?

Or who can say the alphabet backwards contest?

Or a paper airplane building contest?

Or who can memorize the state capitols contest?

The possibilities are endless! Do it!

4. *Choose a Bible verse to memorize each week for the entire family. Announce the verse of the week every Saturday morning and write it on a white board in your kitchen. Put the weekly verse on the bathroom mirror and on every bedroom door. Then, on every Friday afternoon, have each child write out the Bible verse and decorate it with glitter, pieces of fabric and stickers. Insert each child's page into their own 3-ring binder so at the end of the Summer, they will have a beautiful, creative record of the Bible verses of the Summer.*

5. *Teach your children to embrace the fun and purpose found only in giving to someone else. Perhaps you could have a yard sale and give the profits to a missionary. Volunteer, as a family, to paint a Sunday School room at church. Go to a widow's house and weed her flower gardens or wash windows for her. Volunteer, as a family, to baby-sit for a young couple so they can have a date night. Make cards and take them to the residents of a local nursing home.*

   The very best memories you will ever give your children will not be made at Disneyworld, at an exotic beach or even at the neighborhood playground. The very best gift you can give to your children is found in the meaning of serving others and giving to others.

6. *Make a list of interesting and free places to visit within 2 hours of your home. Pack a lunch every Saturday or Sunday and visit these unique places that are within driving distance of where you are raising your family. Make sure that you listen to great music while you drive.*

   Begin with worship music for the first 20 minutes or so.

   Then listen to Broadway Show tunes or Disney songs.

   Introduce culture to your family vehicle with a classical piece or two.

   Every family needs a thorough knowledge of and appreciation for

Patriotic tunes! Sing along to "You're a Grand Old Flag!", "Yankee Doodle Dandy", and "God Bless America!"

How about playing some popular music from your teen-age years?

And as always … make sure to end your day with worship.

Have the youngest members of the family draw a picture of what they saw that day and encourage the school-age children to write a short report of the landmark that you visited.

7. *Buy ice cream from the ice cream truck at least once during the Summer!*

8. *Show a movie for all of the neighborhood kids on the side of your house or garage! Rent or borrow a projector and show a family friendly movie at twilight on a Friday night. Invite all of the families on your street and have them bring lawn chairs and blankets to sit on and snacks to pass around.*

95 days are gone in a flash.

18 Summers disappear like vapor.

The ache that fills my heart every year at one minute past September 23 has little to do with the frost on the morning grass or the vibrant colors of the leaves. The ache is birthed in the knowledge that 18 Summers have come and gone. I'll never have the opportunity again to make blueberry popsicles … lie in the grass and name the clouds with a giggling girl … or catch a salamander with a freckle-faced boy.

95 days. 18 Summers. That's all you get.

BIBLE READING
Psalm 90:12-17 and James 4:14-17

JOYFUL THOUGHTS TO PONDER
If your children are still at home, make a list of things that you would

like to do with them this Summer.

If your children are no longer at home, make a list of the sweet memories that you have from Summers gone by.

If you have never had children, think about some of your childhood Summer memories. Is there anyone that you can share these memories with?

Why is childhood such an important part of a person's life? What are some of the life lessons that you learned during childhood?

_____

_____

_____

The Wonder of YOU!

Mrs. Dombrowski, an Australian war bride, who was also my second grade teacher, wrote this in my second grade yearbook:

> *"This above all: to thine own self be true,*
>
> *And it must follow, as the night, the day,*
>
> *Thou canst not then be false to any man."*

> —WILLIAM SHAKESPEARE

Please! I was only 7 years old! I had no clue what these words were trying to communicate or what Mrs. Dombrowski was thinking!!

Why didn't she choose to quote the esteemed Dr. Seuss?

> *"Today you are you ... that is truer than true.*
>
> *There is no one alive who is youer than you."*

Don't both quotes mean the exact same thing?! Well ... you have to admit ... they are close!

Mrs. Dombrowski, although she never had children of her own, had chosen to convey two very different but oh! such rich possibilities to me ... the little blonde girl who believed that her teacher walked on water.

First of all, Mrs. Dombrowski was instructing me to stretch beyond the simple yet wonderful wisdom of Seuss. She was challenging the 7 year old in me to think like a 10 year old ... or a 14 year old ... or even like an adult.

Secondly, the never-to-be-forgotten Margaret Dombrowski, with the words written in my second grade yearbook, was telling me, "Carol ... I believe in you! You are made for more!"

Now ... I didn't understand Mrs. Dombrowski's chosen Shakespearean quote in the second grade ... nor in the fourth grade ... nor in the sixth grade. But by the time I arrived in Junior High School, I was beginning to understand what my beloved lifetime influencer was endeavoring to say ...

Figure out who you are ... Figure out why you are here ... Figure out what you believe and what you stand for!

Don't just be one of the crowd ... Don't compromise who you are to please others.

Think thoughts bigger than you are able to think on your own ... Stretch your brain!

Do you want to know what I truly believe more than five decades after Mrs. Dombrowski wrote those words in my black and white yearbook? I believe that the brilliant Australian war bride was declaring to an impressionable, wide-eyed daughter of the heart,

"Carol ... any average second grader can enjoy Dr. Seuss with all his quirks and colors and 4 letter words.

But Carol ... you were made for more than average ... you were made for more than above average. You were made to be a person of virtue and character.

Don't give in to the whims of the day and the fads of your culture ... defy whims and fads with well-chosen values and with the commitment to noble character."

And now ... allow me to turn Mrs. Dombrowski's opinion and inescapable challenges in your direction ...

Why are you here?

Why are you still sucking in the atmosphere of planet earth?

Are you here to raise a significant family or perhaps to take care of the elderly? Are you here to run for public office or to take care of the sick? Are you here to teach children to paint ... to sing ... and to pray?

Why are you here?

Do not short-change your life with mediocrity. Any average

person can settle into a rut and be content with mere status quo.

But you were made for more.

You were not made for average… you were made for extraordinary!

Figure out who you are … why you are here … and be passionate about it!

Stand up for something noble! Let your one voice be a resounding voice of excellent values, immovable integrity and passionate kindness.

I know that I know that I know that there is not one *common* person reading these words today. Inside of each one of you lies a seed of greatness. However, … if left unfertilized and unattended … that is all it will ever be … a miniscule, nearly invisible seed of greatness.

It is up to you, as an uncommon gift to this world, to fertilize your great seed, which may currently be lying dormant, with big dreams and with goals both short term and long term.

It is up to you to pull out the weeds around that seed of greatness. Extinguish mediocrity and compromise. Choke selfishness and small thinking before they even have a chance to grow.

Discover why you were born and go for it with every ounce of creativity and passion in your soul! You will make Mrs. Dombrowski proud when you determine not only what you were made to do but more importantly *who you were meant to be.*

And so, my gift to you this brand new day is a quote. Just as the words of Shakespeare were deposited in my innocent soul by a woman of great character and intellect so many years ago, allow me to share with you some soul-shaking words today!

> *"When God wants a great work done in the world or a great wrong righted, He goes about it in a very unusual way. He doesn't stir up His earthquakes or send forth His thunderbolts. Instead, He has a helpless baby born, perhaps in a simple home and of some obscure mother. And then God puts the idea into the mother's heart, and she puts it into the baby's mind. And then God waits. The greatest forces in the world are not the earthquakes and the thunderbolts. The greatest forces in the world are babies."*

—E. T. SULLIVAN

You were that baby born 18 ... 27 ... 32 ... 48 ... 60 or more years ago into which a great idea was deposited. You have more potential than an earthquake or a thunderbolt.

God has been waiting for you to become the force you were made to be!

BIBLE READING
I Corinthians 12:4-31

JOYFUL THOUGHTS TO PONDER
As you do the Bible reading for this week, reflect on the gifts that God has given to you. What are some of the things that you are gifted in? Are you using those gifts?

Mrs. Dombrowski, my second grade teacher, was one of the people who believed in me before I was old enough to even know what the word "potential" meant. Who are the some of the people who believed in you? If they are still living, write them a thank you note this week.

Is there a younger person in whom you see great potential? Spend some time praying for that person today and then either write them a note or tell them in person what you see in his or her young life.

Why are you here?

_____

_____

_____

Prayer ... It's All I Have

"Now He was telling them a parable to show them at all times they should pray and not lose heart."

—LUKE 18:1

I long to be a prayer warrior. I want to live in that influential place of heartfelt communication and sweet communion with God.

Prayer is the force that makes Hell quiver in fear and causes Heaven to stand to its feet with joyful applause.

I know it deep within my soul.

Nothing eternal is accomplished on earth without the power and focus of a saint who is committed to the discipline of prayer.

I know that I know that I know.

Prayer is the vehicle through which the greatest work of my life will be done.

I absolutely know it.

"Therefore I say to you, all things for which you pray and ask, believe that you have received them, and they will be granted you."

—MARK 11:12

Why do I feel so bad at it then? Time after time after time, I feel like a failure in the arena of prayer.

I long for my prayers to move mountains, to calm storms and to heal sick people. I long for it day after endless day.

And yet ... day after day after day ... all I see is one mountain range after another. And over all of my mountains, there always seems to be at least one fierce and defiant storm brewing.

What is it with prayer and me?! What is it with prayer and anybody?!

> *"Be anxious for nothing, but in everything by prayer and supplication with thanksgiving let your requests be made known to God. And the peace of God, which surpasses all comprehension, will guard your hearts and your minds in Christ Jesus."*
>
> —PHILIPPIANS 4: 6 & 7

I must tell you ... I refuse to give up. I refuse to be paralyzed or crippled by what my eyes see. I will pray when others give up. I will pray in spite of a quiet Heaven.

I will pray.

I will pray when storms sneer and when mountains mock.

I will pray.

> *"Pray without ceasing."*
>
> —I THESSALONIANS 5:17

I defiantly refuse to believe that prayer is a waste of time. I will set my resolve and pray on when nothing changes.

I will pray in the dark of the night when the towering mountains minimize my value.

I will pray when the howl of life's storms threatens to drown out the volume of my solitary and desperate prayer.

I will pray in the face of sickness and pain. I will beg for God's sweet presence to heal and restore.

> *"In the same way the Spirit also helps our weakness; for we do not know how to pray as we should, but the Spirit Himself intercedes for us with groanings too deep for words; and He who searches the*

hearts knows what the mind of the Spirit is, because He intercedes for the saints according to the will of God."

—ROMANS 8:26 & 27

It's all I have. Prayer is all I have. It's the only power with any potential of making even a temporary difference.

I will wear out the carpet beside my bed with the pressure and insistence of two middle-aged knees whose resolve has been set. Nothing will move me from the battle that takes place from this position.

Nothing.

"Then you will call upon Me and come and pray to Me, and I will listen to you."

—JEREMIAH 29:12

I will get up in the morning with worship in my heart and a prayer on my lips.

I will choose to pray rather than worry as I fold laundry, dash to the grocery store and answer e-mails.

I will lay my head down at night with the determination that any day is a magnificent day that has been given to prayer.

"To this end also we pray for you always, that our God will count you worthy of your calling, and fulfill every desire for goodness and the work of faith with power, so that the name of our Lord Jesus will be glorified in you, and you in Him, according to the grace of our God and the Lord Jesus Christ."

—II THESSALONIANS 1:1

My calling is to prayer. It is my life's work.

God's responsibility and response is to answer and to move.

When I pray, my desires are fulfilled in Him and not in the magical change of situations, circumstances or events. When I pray there is a mighty work that is done in me ... it is a work of faith and power.

I will stand in faith and continue to believe for the miraculous change of situations, circumstances and events. And while I stand, I will pray on. It's my calling, remember?

While my prayers may not change a situation, I now know that my prayers will indeed change me.

When I pray, Jesus in glorified in me and I am glorified in Him.

When I pray, His grace is lavishly dispersed into my world.

I have learned that you don't have to be "good" at prayer for prayer to be "good" in you.

I now know that in order to be good at prayer ... you just have to mean it. And I do. I mean it so very much.

> *"Pray then, in this way:*
>
> *Our Father who is in Heaven, Hallowed be Your name.*
>
> *Your kingdom come. Your will be done, On earth as it is in Heaven.*
>
> *Give us this day our daily bread,*
>
> *and forgive us our debts, as we also have forgiven our debtors.*
>
> *And do not lead us into temptation, but deliver us from evil.*
>
> *For Yours is the kingdom and the power and the glory forever. Amen."*

—MATTHEW 6:9-13

BIBLE READING
Colossians 1:1-12

JOYFUL THOUGHTS TO PONDER
Perhaps this would be a good week for you to start a prayer journal if

you don't already have one. Make a list of the people that you want to pray for on a daily basis and on a weekly basis. Be sure that you leave space to write in the answers to prayer as well!

What are some of the ways that God has answered you when you pray? Does He always say, "Yes!" to your prayers? Why or why not?

What does it mean to "pray the will of God"?

_____

_____

_____

Overwhelmed

Does your heart ever feel overwhelmed?

Are you disheartened by your inability to meet everyone's demands and expectations?

Some days my heart vacillates between being raw with paralyzing frustration and simultaneously stimulated by a thousand agitations.

In the midst of my obsessive mental processing and impaired human emotions, I starkly realize that in the insistent whirlwind of life, I still have so much for which to be grateful.

Yet continuously ... the floods of demands, disciplines, people, habits, chores, vices and commitments create a massive quagmire in my life that can only be described by one desperate word, *"overwhelming"*!

The call of life is just so deafeningly loud sometimes ...

David the worshipper ... the man after God's own heart ... shared my incompetence at dealing well with all that life dishes out.

"Hear my cry, O God; Give heed to my prayer.

From the end of the earth I call to You when my heart is overwhelmed;

Lead me to the rock that is higher than I.

For You have been a refuge for me, a tower of strength against the enemy.

Let me dwell in Your tent forever;

Let me take refuge in the shelter of Your wings."

—PSALM 61:1-4

Although I do not know what specifically overwhelms you, I can assure you that though the source of your staggering obstacles may look much different than mine, the answer for both of us is the same.

"Hear my cry, O God! Give heed to my prayer."

When you are overwhelmed, take it from David: the first thing you need to do is cry out to God. We need prayer more than we need our circumstances to change. Just going to my infinitely gracious God, Who is lovingly attentive in all of His ways, reminds me that I am not in charge. There is Someone mightier and more powerful than I am Who is well able to bring relief to my mountain of stress.

"From the end of the earth I call to You, when my heart is overwhelmed!"

There is no sin in calling out to God when you are completely and utterly overwhelmed.

The sin would actually be in turning to other less satisfying options. Have you ever mistakenly believed that spending, eating, being entertained, going to the spa or responding with your emotions is what you need to conquer the overwhelming circumstances and events of your life? Those things are deceptive distractions and possess all the healing power of a miniscule Band-aid following open-heart surgery.

"Lead me to the rock that is higher than I ..."

The second word of advice that is discernable in David's prayer is that we all need God to lead us. We need Him to take us by our human hands and then to guide us with His divine hands to a higher place. He always wisely leads His children to a more secure vantage point than the circumstances of life are able to offer. The benefit of standing on a Rock that is "higher than I", is that it places me above my circumstances and therefore I am able to see from Heaven's perspective.

One of the most destructive mistakes that any of us make during moments of overwhelming madness is to be led by our emotions. Anger and impatience will do damage to relationships that may be difficult to repair. I must humbly realize that my emotions often lie to me but God will lead me in triumph even in overwhelming times ... especially in overwhelming times.

"For You have been a refuge for me, a tower of strength against the enemy ..."

When you are feeling overwhelmed, focus not on what is causing the irritation or annoyance but begin to declare Who God is. Remove your eyes from your circumstances and set your mind, mouth and gaze on the only One Who is able to help you! God is your safe place and will strongly protect you against the enemy forces of busyness, difficult relationships, a failing economy, health challenges and priorities. He is more than able!

"Let me dwell in Your tent forever; Let me take refuge in the shelter of Your wings."

There is no safer, more peaceful place to be than abiding in Him and with Him. When I linger in His presence and enjoy the safety of His Word, it is at that moment that the overwhelming things of this earth truly grow strangely dim. When His nearness overshadows all that screeches my name, I am at peace at last. The life that He gives is the life that I have dreamed about and longed for.

His presence miraculously empowers me to face another day of the demanding details of life. The Word of God powerfully protects and shields me from the rapid fire of life's demands. Prayer helps me to wisely focus on that which is eternal and not on that which merely stirs up a ruckus.

So ... the next time that you or I find ourselves in similar and overwhelming circumstances ... let's not walk but run to Him and all that He is! I resolve to take a break from this mad, mad, mad, mad world and to set my heart where it has always belonged ... in Him.

While others are juggling the voices, the tirade and the insistence of this temporary world, I will be the one with my hands in air, gaze fixed on Heaven and crying with gut-wrenching desperation, "HELP!"

BIBLE READING

Psalm 61 and 62

JOYFUL THOUGHTS TO PONDER

Why do we often focus on the problem rather than on the power of God?

What benefit does it bring to your life to focus on God rather than on the problem?

What are some of the things in life that are overwhelming to you today? Can you think of a Bible verse that applies to that overwhelming circumstance?

Difficult People

Do you ever wonder why God allows difficult people into your life?

I must admit, my emotions would be 99.9% perfect if it weren't for people!!

Difficult, frustrating people barge into my peaceful world and disrupt my stability with their instability! The nerve of difficult people!

Why can't I just meet Pollyanna, Santa Claus and Mother Theresa along my life's journey? Why does my life seem to be filled with the Grinch, Barney Fife and an ugly stepsister or two?!

Have you ever had a friendship with someone and then used these words to describe your relationship, "Well, she just brings out the worst in me!" Hopefully … you are not saying this about your spouse … or your parents … or the people you work with … or your siblings … or your children!

I have come to realize that often God places difficult people in my life not to bring out the worst in me … but to bring out the best in me!

Perhaps the reason that the Lord allows our lives to collide with difficult people is not to bring out the "selfish" in us … but to bring out the Jesus in us.

It is when I am trying to build a relationship with a fractious person that I must rely not upon my own natural inclinations and preferences but I must stay on my knees and pray for the fruit of the Spirit to be mine in abundance.

I believe that when Jesus wants to strengthen our ability to love, to encourage, and to comfort He sends a difficult person into our lives … special delivery from Heaven!

I think that what scares me about this entire philosophy is that I just might be someone else's difficult person! Now … that's a sobering thought indeed.

God, in His infinite wisdom and goodness, challenges me to love the unlovable … to care for someone who spits in my eye … and to talk kindly about someone who has ruined my reputation with their gossip. God loves me when I am at my very worst – and He calls me in every situation and with every relationship to be like Him. His plan for my life is that I would be less like the human version of me … and more like the loving version of Him.

> *"Therefore be imitators of God, as beloved children, and walk in love, just as Christ also loved you and gave Himself up for us, an offering and a sacrifice to God as a fragrant aroma."*
>
> —EPHESIANS 5:1 & 2

When you walk in love and choose to be kind rather than throw an emotional tantrum, you are saying, "I will act like my Dad! I have the family gene that enables me to love difficult people! It's what Christians do!!"

When you imitate God and love your husband … smile at your ornery neighbor and listen to your loquacious sister … you smell good! You don't smell like verbal vomit but your life becomes a sweet aroma that wafts up into the nostrils of God.

When we respond with heartfelt love to others' dysfunction, I have a feeling that God, the Father, is smiling down from Heaven and proudly declaring, "Look at my delightful child! She is acting just like Me!"

> *"But I say to you, love your enemies and pray for those who persecute you."*
>
> —MATTHEW 5:44

This particular verse calls us not to respond with emotion to the difficult people in our lives but to respond with love and with prayer. God has created you at this time in history to be a conduit of His love and He has pointed your life straight toward fussy, irritable people.

God sent His Son, Jesus, into the world because we were the difficult people who needed forgiveness and love. Don't allow difficult people to rock your boat emotionally or to steal your peace and joy. But allow people to bring out the family resemblance in you... because after all ... you do look just like your Dad!

BIBLE READING

Ephesians 4:17-32

JOYFUL THOUGHTS TO PONDER

Make a list of the difficult people in your life. Now, pray for them and ask God to help you love these people like He loves them!

Make a list of the lovable people in your life. Now, pray for these friends and ask God to help you love these people like He loves them!

What are some of the character traits that difficult people have brought out in you?

What are some of the character traits that lovable people have brought out in you?

_____

_____

_____

The Elusive Nature of Time

Time ... where does it go?

The most valuable commodity that we have been given as human beings is the gift of time: ... of minutes ... of hours ... of days.

It seems like only yesterday I was looking forward to my senior year of High School and now I am a grandmother. When did that happen?!

When did I graduate from playing with Barbie dolls and practicing piano to being a bride ... and then a mother ... and now a grandmother? When did that happen?!

When did my raucous, noisy, messy nest get so empty? When did that happen? ... tell me when.

It happened in a thousand yesterdays that are filled with the memories of cherished friendships ... bittersweet good-byes ... the echoes of laughter ... and the daily reminders of what is truly important in life.

The scrapbook of my heart is filled with a collage of moments too precious to verbalize and too valuable to calculate in earthly economy.

As I flip through the intangible pages of the days that have been given to me, I realize that some days were wasted with impatience and disappointment. It is never a good day that is taken over by human frustration or disillusionment.

I have wasted time being angry at a person made in the image of God and being depressed over situations and events over which I had absolutely no control.

Who do I think I am?!

I have frittered away days spent in the worry of something that never happened and in the fear of the shadow ghosts of weakness. What a colossal waste!

I have misused the treasure of an extraordinary day by spewing the venom of my heart on the lives of people whom I love dearly. I am ashamed.

The untold wealth in this cherished peek into the past also holds the abundance of all that has been meaningful in my life.

I am amazed that I was given the delight of raising 5 little lives for the Kingdom of God! After so many years of barrenness and infertility, of standing in faith and begging God for more, He opened the windows of Heaven and blew joy in my direction.

I loved every minute of peanut butter and jelly kisses ... of paper dolls and birthday cakes ... of choo-choo trains and baseball games. Those were the best days ... the days that mattered ... the pieces of gold in my life.

I have loved being best friends with my mom. How I wish that you could know her! A woman of excellence and humor! A woman who prays and believes and prays some more.

I loved falling in love with Craig and realizing that he was "the one". He has always been a man of honor ... a man whom I could trust ... and a man after God's own heart. What have I ever done to deserve this man whose heart is pure gold?

Time ... where does it go? Oh! How I want to live well the rest of the days that have been given to me by the calendar of Heaven's bounty.

I want to spend my days encouraging people and writing thank you notes.

I want to invest my days believing for the best and not giving in to disillusionment or despair. A very wise man once told me, "It's more fun to believe!"

I want to lavish in the laughter of children, to wade in the gift of extraordinary friends and to drown in the beauty of creation.

I want to be kind to cantankerous and fractious people. When I have chosen to love and be generous in the face of personal cruelty and gossip, I have created a day that God Himself would applaud!

Life is too dear and much too fleeting to waste the glory of one ordinary day. I will not waste this life. Not one day. Not one hour. Not one minute.

I will pray for miracles and I will also look for the opportunity to be someone else's miracle.

I now understand that tomorrow's memories are being created today. And so, I resolve, this day, to splash extravagantly in the joy of His presence.

BIBLE READING
Psalm 71

JOYFUL THOUGHTS TO PONDER

What has been the most joyful season of your life so far? What has made it joy-filled?

What can you do to bring more joy to the current season of life that you are in?

What are some of the spiritual and practical disciplines that you can incorporate into your life to "wring the joy out of an ordinary day"?

Choose a friend who can be your accountant in this. Hold one another accountable to the promise that neither of you will waste the days that you have been given but that you will use every day to glorify Christ. Who is this accountant in your life?

_____

_____

_____

The Blessing of Closed Doors

I often pray a prayer that starts like this, "God, open a door that only YOU can open!" How I love the God Who opens doors ... doors of opportunity ... doors of relationship ... doors of ministry ... doors of destiny.

But, I must tell you, I have been pondering lately my extreme gratitude that God has loved me enough to close at least as many doors for me as He has opened.

As I look back at my life from a vantage point of 6 decades ... I am just as grateful for the doors that God has strategically kept closed as I am for the ones that He has deliberately opened.

I am grateful for the many times (shamefully too many!) that God closed a door on a relationship during my dating years. Can you relate?

How grateful I am that God chose a kind, committed man of God for me and didn't allow me to choose based on teen-age hormones or young adult selfishness. How different my life would be today if God had allowed me to push open a door of my own choosing rather than of His Divine Will.

> *"God, thank You for loving me enough NOT to give in to my demands and whims. Forgive me for being flirtatious, for nursing a broken heart or two and for questioning whether You knew best or not."*

I am grateful that God gently held doors of destiny closed tightly for me until the right season in life.

I am grateful that during my years of mothering the doors to publishing contracts remained firmly closed so that I could focus on the 5 most important things in my life. Impressionable hearts ... fingerprints on every window ... bedtime stories ... PBJ sandwiches and little arms around my neck. The five children that I was allowed to raise are now my greatest masterpieces.

If I write hundreds of best-selling books, each one will pale in comparison to the call of raising 5 world-changing children.

> *"God, thank You for loving me enough to keep doors of opportunity closed tightly until the fullness of Your time. Forgive me for not trusting You during those years of waiting."*

I am grateful that I don't always get to live where I want to live but where God needs me to live. I would rather be serving the Kingdom of God on the frozen tundra than living a life of opulence and relaxation on the most elite beach in the world.

> *God, Your ways are highest and best. Forgive me for complaining about the weather, about the location and about the living conditions. I want YOU more than I want things or stuff."*

I am grateful that God's ways truly are higher than my ways ... and He knows what doors to miraculously open ... and what doors to patiently keep closed.

I do believe that there are times that I must persevere in prayer for the best doors to be opened for me and for those that I love.

Some doors remained unopened simply because I don't stay on my knees long enough ... or often enough. There are some doors that have remained regretfully closed just because of my lack of persistence in prayer.

And for those closed doors, I repent and pray again. I ask God to give me the resolve of Daniel ... of Joseph ... and of Hannah.

I ask God to give me the focus of Paul ... and Peter ... and John.

I ask God to give me the fortitude of Hannah ... and Esther ... and Ruth.

I have learned that it is only in the prayer closet of my heart that I discover which doors were never meant to be opened ... and which doors I must prayer harder and longer about.

It is in the prayer closet of my heart that I experience the power of God ... Who always opens the best doors for me.

It is in the prayer closet of my heart that I relinquish the doorknob of all of my future doors ... and safely place my hand in His.

> *"Devote yourselves to prayer, keeping alert in it with an attitude of thanksgiving; praying at the same time for me as well, that God will open up to me a door for the word, so that I may speak forth the mystery of Christ."*

—COLOSSIANS 4:2 & 3

BIBLE READING

I Corinthians 16:5-10; Colossians 4:2-6 and Revelation 3:7-8

JOYFUL THOUGHTS TO PONDER

What are some of the principles that the Holy Spirit showed you through the Bible readings this week?

What doors has God miraculously opened for you?

What doors has God kept shut for you? Do you see His protection in closing these doors or has it been frustrating?

What is the one door that you wish that God would open for you? Pray about it and then trust Him with the answer.

_____

_____

_____

At The Beach... With Jesus

"That day Jesus went out of the house and was sitting by the sea. And large crowds gathered to Him, so He got into a boat and sat down, and the whole crowd was standing on the beach."

—MATTHEW 13:1 & 2

Have you ever been to the beach? The beach is most definitely my "happy place"!

Every morning, when I wake up at the beach, the first thing that I do is to walk outside and just listen ... and then look.

Some days the ocean is turbulent and angry with white caps and high, threatening waves.

Other days, the surface of the ocean looks like glass - glorious in its hues of emerald green and peacock blue.

I love the sounds at the beach. The never-ending call of the ocean surf reminds me that God never changes. He is always calling my name ... trying to capture my attention. God is relentless in his pursuit of me and the perpetual motion of the waves remind me of His eternal perspective on my life.

Often, when I go to the beach, the weather is cold and so I am not able to sit on the beach and soak up the sunshine. During those winter days at the beach, I take long, luxurious walks on the beach as a daily ritual. I walk for miles and miles listening ... watching ... and praying.

With rolled up sweat pants, hands dug deeply into sweatshirt pockets, I meander along the shoreline. Often my feet are absolutely numb by the time I return to the vacation home but my heart is always alive and warm!

I am filled to overflowing with the grandeur of creation and with a God Who loved me enough to create a beach!

Some days, my husband, Craig, joins me for my daily walks where ocean meets land. When he does this during the winter months, I know that he does it as a gift to me because it's really cold … I stay out way too long … and he likes the beach … but he doesn't LOVE the beach the way that I do.

Some days we talk as we walk … other days we just walk.

One late afternoon, when Craig and I were out on our daily beach pilgrimage, we talked about 2 things that I want to share with you … so join us … roll up your pant legs and get ready for the ocean surf to splash upon your soul.

"I have noticed that there are different types of homes on the beach," I remarked to Craig. "On this end of the beach, the homes are worth millions of dollars, aren't they?"

"At least a million," said my dashing, no-nonsense husband.

"As you travel down further toward the west," I continued, "the homes seem to be simpler and worth less, don't you think?"

"That's a nice way of putting it, Carol," he responded. "I would call them run-down. Some of them are not much more than shacks."

"But do you know what they have in common?" I persisted. "Do you know what is the same with both the multi-million dollar homes and the shacks?"

"Tell me," Craig said with his ocean-blue eyes penetrating my soul.

"They all have the same view," I imparted. "It doesn't matter how much money the people have spent to live here … they all see the same ocean. The same sand. The same sunsets."

My talkative husband was quiet and smiled as he thought about it. We didn't need to talk anymore that day. We both knew what God was speaking to us.

Our view of life has been spectacular!

The next day we walked east along the shoreline so that as we turned toward our home for the week, we would be walking west and thus see the sunset.

Craig was kicking the sand like a little boy and I was just enjoying the moment. The sun ... the white sand ... the depth of the ocean's colors ... the roar of the waves.

I smiled at the heavens and said to Craig, "Did you know that this is one of my very favorite things to do in all of life? I love walking on the beach. I love everything about it. My heart is so happy. It's right up there with Christmas music," I said impishly.

My thoughtful husband replied, "What are your favorite things to do in the whole world?"

Well ...I didn't need to think long about **that** very long or very hard ... this is what I said ...

Reading my Bible ...
   Teaching the Word of God ...
      Worshipping the Lord passionately and with reckless abandon

Being with my children and grandchildren ...
   Preparing for Christmas ...
      Talking to my mom ...

Reading a great book ...
   Writing a great book ...

Listening to timeless music ...
   The great hymns of the faith and contemporary songs of praise
      the masterpieces of classic composers
         the scores from musicals and Broadway show tunes

Filling my soul with the glory of creation ...
   walking on the beach ...

Then ... I looked at my husband with a twinkle in my eye and remarked to this great theologian of a man, "You know, I am a lot like Jesus ... because He loved the beach, too!"

We both laughed and kept walking toward the sunset. The imprints of our feet were erased in the evening tide and our laughter was swallowed in the roar of the waves.

But our lives and our faith were both renewed in the joy of the day... in the glory of the moment in the security of love and in the Reason we live.

BIBLE READING

Psalm 8

JOYFUL THOUGHTS TO PONDER

Where is your "happy place"?

What are your favorite things to do in the whole world?! Make a long list of these things! Hold nothing back!

How do you renew your faith and your joy? What restores your soul?

_____

_____

_____

The Twelve-Year-Old You

What would you say to the 12-year-old **you**?

What are the valuable lessons that you wish you would have known at 12 years old?

It's a good question ... isn't it?

If I could talk to the 12 year old in you ... and in me ... this is what I would say. This is a compilation of the wisdom that I sorely wish someone would have told me when I was 12.

How I wish I could save the 12-year-old Carol from making some of the mistakes that I have made along life's journey!

How I wish I could have challenged that blue-eyed pile of emotion and potential to be more than she ever dreamed of being!

And so ... to the 12 year old Carol ...

1. It really is more important to be kind than to be pretty. People will forget how you dressed for a certain occasion, what color eye shadow you wear and how often you get your hair cut. But they will never forget your heart. They will long remember and be impacted by your genuine kindness and friendship.

2. Don't date in High School ... it is a total waste of time. Focus on things in High School other than the opposite sex. Develop Godly relationships with other girls. Reach out to girls who are being bullied and be their true friend. Go on Missions trips. Teach Sunday school. But please don't give your heart to a string of hormonally charged males who care more about how you look than who you are. Wait for the right man at the right time. He is

worth the wait ... trust me ... I know.

3. Practice the piano or take gymnastics lessons. Keep playing soccer and writing in your journal. Study ballet and learn to give speeches. So often when the teen-age years and hormones hit, girls become distracted from their childhood dreams. Don't allow your dreams or the disciplines of your little girl years to become lost in the foolishness of parties, social media and dating.

4. Keep in touch with your childhood and High School friends. That sweet Girl Scout song holds a lifetime of truth in it, *"Make new friends, but keep the old; one is silver and the other gold."* There is absolutely nothing like going out for lunch with someone who has known you from the inside out since you were 8 or 10 or 12.

5. Hold your babies ... they grow up so quickly. Someday you really will meet the man of your dreams ... and you really will have babies together ... and you really will be a mom. When that day comes, remember that the bonding process that takes place during the newborn days is more valuable than a beautiful nursery, designer clothes or a full night's sleep. Rock your babies ... sing to them ... hold them ... snuggle them ... pray over them. These really are the most precious moments of your entire life.

6. Increase your vocabulary. Listen to the words that other people speak and make a list of the words that are unfamiliar to you. Look up the meanings of the words and try to incorporate them into your daily speech. There is nothing quite as captivating as a vocabulary that is not peppered with slang but is filled with the beauty of interesting words and enriching phrases.

7. Don't just read the twaddle of the day. Travel to England between the pages of "Sense and Sensibility" and "Pride and Prejudice". Experience other times and places through the magic of great literature. Go to the Civil War in "Gone with the Wind" and through the pages of "Little Women". The passport of your mind is too valuable to stay merely in one country and in one time period. Linger over a cup of tea with Ruth Graham in her biography, "A Portrait of Ruth" and travel to China with Amy Carmichael in "God's Missionary". The world is so much bigger than your little corner of it ... so envelop yourself in meaningful literature that will

enlarge your capacity to dream. Trust me ... I know.

8. Listen more than you talk. Women have a horrible habit of talking more than listening. Don't be that girl. Ask questions of others and then truly care about their answers. Don't feel that you have to say everything you think, feel and believe but be someone else's safe place.

9. Don't always drive on the Interstate ... take back roads as often as you can. Arriving at your chosen destination in the shortest possible time is not nearly as important as seeing the beauty along the way. Stop at an old bookstore ... buy lemonade from a child ... walk through an old cemetery and read the tombstones ... linger over a well-tended garden.

10. Respect your parents in every season of life. Listen to their wisdom and never discount their input. You really don't know better than your parents. The world and your peers will tell you to mock them, tolerate them, disobey them, ignore them and sass them. God calls girls from every generation and every historical juncture to honor them. I don't think that you have a better idea than God.

11. Please dress modestly. Please!! Your body is not a show and tell stage for the world to gawk at! Your body was not meant to be paraded for every boy to see what you have been given. Pieces of your underwear should never be easily seen under your shirt, skirt, or shorts. You may think that jeans with rips around your private areas are stylish ... they are not. They are seductive. You can be stylish without being sexy. I dare you! Try to do it! Be a young woman of virtue who refuses to cave into the culture. Have a backbone when it comes to how you dress ... be lovely and not lascivious. (This is a word that you are going to have to look up! See #6 and follow the instructions there! You can do it ... this is a word that you do not want used to describe you!)

12. And please ... don't gossip! Don't be a drama queen! The circumstances and events that you are going through today will quickly pass. Pray your way through every situation and allow God to give you peace. When you talk about others ... let it always be in a kind and encouraging way. When others are

gossiping ... think of something good to say about the victim of their verbal abuse. Your words hold power and with your words you either wound someone or encourage someone. Who do you want to be?

13. Remind yourself on a daily basis that it really does pay to serve God. He has better plans for you than you can even imagine.

14. Choose Godly friends who dress modestly, obey their parents and refuse to gossip or be drama queens. Your life will be better for it.

15. Read your Bible every day. Connect your soul to eternity through this one simple, yet life-altering, choice. You can never underestimate the power of reading a Psalm a day ... a Proverb a day ... or about the life of Jesus Christ every day. If you desire to be the very best version of "you" imaginable ... you will read your Bible.

There are days that I wish I could be 12 years old again and anchor myself to these solid principles that somehow eluded me the first time around. However, we all only get to do life one time. We all only have one chance to be 12 ... and 16 ... and 23 ... and 37 ... and 45 ... and 58.

And so today I will hunker down once again into the important stuff in life and be the very best version of "me" possible. While my feet yet remain on the soil of planet earth, of worldly culture and of a civilization that touts compromise, I will maintain my focus on all that is glorious and eternal.

I will purpose to set this heart, in every season of life, on that which is noble and pure and righteous.

> *"Finally, sisters, whatever is true, whatever is honorable, whatever is just, whatever is pure, whatever is lovely, whatever is commendable, if there is any excellence, if there is anything worthy of praise, dwell on these things."*
>
> —PHILIPPIANS 4:8

BIBLE READING

Proverbs 31

JOYFUL THOUGHTS TO PONDER

What would you tell the 12-year-old **you**?

What is the most valuable lesson your mother or grandmother taught you?

Who is a woman whom you have admired over the years? What is it that you have admired about her? If she is still living, why don't you write her a note and tell her of your gratitude?

_____

_____

_____

Ain't Life Grand?!

It's the little things that make life grand, isn't it?!

A glass of iced tea on the back deck ...
The sweet giggle of a delicious child ...
A kind text message from a friend who lives far away ...

The smell of fresh-cut grass ...
A good book and a cup of coffee ...
Dinner at a friend's house ...

So often, in my life, I have made the mistake of living for the big moments ... for the red-letter days of promotions, bonuses and celebrations, when, in reality, those giant occasions are not what life is made of at all.

Life, at its finest, is built upon heartfelt smiles ...
Long walks on a country road ...
An unexpected phone call from a loved one ...

If graduations, publishing contracts, and standing ovations were the building blocks of a rich and meaningful life ... my life would be tenuous and without much foundational support.

But because the real stuff of life is as close and as dear as the morning song of the bird out my kitchen window ... the companionship of my daughter on my daily run ...and the treasure of reading a well-loved devotional book ... I find my life to be a rich repository of all that is good and substantive.

The glory of applause is momentary ... the accolades of achievement are fleeting ... the once in a lifetime events are rare ...

but it is the simple pleasures that give life sparkle and joy.

If high-power business meetings and hall of fame moments are what you have built a life upon … perhaps you need a new architectural plan. If you live for the adrenaline rush that only championship games and trips to Hawaii bring … perhaps your adrenaline is bought at too high a price.

> *"Make sure that your character is free from the love of money, being content with what you have; for He Himself has said, "I will never desert you, nor will I ever forsake you."*
>
> —HEBREWS 13:5

Paul reminds all of us … in every generation … to learn the contentment that is found not in achieving but in belonging. Contentment is a learned behavior and not a knee-jerk reaction to life. Contentment requires choosing … listening … processing … and submitting oneself to the miracle of an ordinary day.

> *" … For I have learned to be content in whatever circumstances I am."*
>
> —PHILIPPIANS 4:11

When I look back at the substance of living that created a healthy childhood for my children, I realize that it was popsicles on a hot Summer day … laughing at a shared family joke … and praying every night before bed that brought security and happiness into our home.

Oh … we cheered like fanatics at the championship ball games … I cried at five High School graduations … and we celebrated every birthday like royalty … but those moments did not define the life we had been given.

What made life worthwhile at 8120 Stillbreeze Drive was reading a book together in the evenings … and catching fireflies in the backyard … and singing around the piano. Those simple yet valuable choices gave us a strong foundation of life at its finest and its richest.

Perhaps living inside a regular day in which nothing of earth-moving significance happens is at the heart of all that is truly meaningful and extraordinary.

The glory of life is found quite simply in the ordinary moments. The treasure of a life well lived is acquired not in getting but in giving. The substance of all that is good and rich and meaningful is found in a thousand minute gifts that are easily overlooked if one is not careful.

Rather than looking for gold at the end of the rainbow ... enjoy the rainbow.

Rather than aching for your baby's first step ... enjoy his or her little arms around your neck for one more day.

Rather than emphasizing the importance of performance-based living ... be content with the company of those you love the most and know the best.

Play peek-a-boo with the little person across the restaurant ...

Take a bouquet of flowers to a widow from church ...

Meet a High School friend for lunch ...

It is the truly important stuff of life!

BIBLE READING

Hebrews 13:1-8

JOYFUL THOUGHTS TO PONDER

What does the word "contentment" mean to you?

What has brought contentment into your life?

What is your idea of a perfect day?

_____

_____

_____

The Dread of What Lies Ahead

Autumn must be the most glorious of months. I look out of my window and see the green grass of Summer now scattered with the brilliance of red, yellow and orange leaves.

The placid geese of the Summer that I encounter on my daily walk are now showing off. They are skidding across the pond with a magnificent demonstration of splash and strength as they prepare for the long journey ahead.

A drive through the countryside holds more inspiration and beauty than the finest art gallery in the world. The hills are ablaze with a riot of color that no human paintbrush could reveal.

If autumn is so miraculous ... then why do I dread it so much? Why does my heart constrict in pain every time I see another leaf fall to the ground and hear another goose honk its travel plans over my home?!

It's because I cringe at the very thought that snowflakes are not too far away. Winter is NOT my best friend ... and the thought of mountains of snow, frigid temperatures and the absence of Mr. Sunshine chills me to the bone.

I have a problem. I have allowed my distress at the onslaught of winter to rob me of the joy of today. And tomorrow. And an entire season of the year! It's time for me to grab control of my out-of-control emotions and embrace the joy of today.

For you ... it might not be the dread of the coldest of seasons that denies you the joy of the moment but it might be something else.

Perhaps you cringe at the thought of a child preparing for college and so you cry your way through their senior year. Perhaps you have sobbed uncontrollably at the last football game and forget the victories won. Maybe you have blubbered through choir concerts, teachers' conferences and packing the final sack lunches.

You might be dreading the last few days of the pre-school years and so rather than celebrate all that is ahead, you pore through baby books and wipe your tears with receiving blankets.

Perhaps you shudder when contemplating your looming retirement from a career that was fulfilling and challenging. Rather than crafting a plan to continue valuable friendships you find yourself withdrawing from the camaraderie of the workplace into a sullen shell.

What is it with us?! We can just be so horribly human at times!

This is what I have come to realize ... God has been to my future and it is good! He is working every event and circumstance of my life for my highest good and His greatest glory just because I love Him.

There is not a day in life that is worth dreading or withdrawing from. Every day is a gift ... an extraordinary gift. There is no such thing as an "ordinary" day or even a "bad" day when you are living for a purpose greater than your own.

Whether you are shoveling snow or planting flowers ... whether you are changing diapers or waving good-bye ... whether you are up and at 'em at the crack of dawn or can spend a leisurely morning over a cup of coffee and good book ... remind yourself that life is a gift.

Every day is a rare and priceless treasure that is meant to be valued not dreaded. I will not waste one day. Not one hour. Not one minute. I will never again take for granted the joy of a glorious day.

I am determined to live well today. I am committed to embracing every day of this miracle known as "life" with passion and with gusto. How about you? Will you put away your dread ... your fear ... your anxieties ... and your regrets? Will you dive into a life that was meant to be experienced with wholehearted laughter and delight?!

It is the deepest hope and prayer of my heart that you will decide that today is worth celebrating no matter what is behind you or what looms in front of you. And ... while you are deciding ... will you excuse me? I need to go ...

There are some geese outside my window putting on a show that deserves my full attention!

BIBLE READING
Philippians 3:7-14

JOYFUL THOUGHTS TO PONDER
What are some events in life that you enjoy remembering?

What are some events in life that you need to leave behind and forget?

What does it mean to *"press on toward the goal for the prize of the upward call of God in Christ Jesus"*?

_____

_____

_____

Give Me Another Mountain!

Joshua and Caleb. Leaders. Warriors. Obeyers. Mountain-moving men.

Who were these ancient men named Joshua and Caleb? What do they have to do with your life ... and my life ... today?

Joshua and his buddy, Caleb, were sent into the Promised Land along with 10 other men to spy out the land. Moses, their statesman and leader, told these 12 courageous men to bring back a report. Moses wanted to know exactly what and who occupied the land to which the people of God had been assigned.

While the 10 companions of Joshua and Caleb only saw the giants and the impossibilities in the land ... Joshua and Caleb saw the infinite size of their God and the eternal power of His might!

> *"Then Caleb quieted the people before Moses and said, 'We should by all means go up and take possession of it, for we will surely overcome it.'*
>
> *But the men who had gone up with him, said, 'We are not able to go up against the people, for they are too strong for us.'*
>
> *So they gave out to the sons of Israel a bad report of the land which they had spied out, saying, 'The land through which we have gone, in spying it out, is a land that devours its inhabitants; and all the people whom we saw in it are men of great size ... we became like grasshoppers in our own sight and so we were in their sight.'"*
>
> —NUMBERS 13:30-33

The 10 men who walked by sight and not by faith saw only their personal weakness and lack. Caleb and Joshua only saw the possibilities of serving God in this new land of opportunity and promise!

The behemoth human beings that Joshua and Caleb saw with their very own eyes were not intimidating to them. They were more focused on and in awe of the God Whom they had chosen to serve.

Joshua and Caleb realized what you and I often miss ... we each have a choice as we take new territory for the Kingdom of God. Will we walk by sight? Or will we walk by faith?

Will the giants in the enemy's territory determine our perception of who will win? Or will our flint-like gaze cast upon the power of God determine our courage and resolute faith?

Joshua knew that the giants of the land would be an easy prey for the people of God. Joshua declared, in the face of insurmountable odds,

"The Lord is with us ... do not fear them."

—NUMBERS 14:9B

This man, Joshua, in his lifetime won too many battles to count. He led the people of God into the blessings and victories of the Promised Land. Oh, Joshua fought battles along the way but he overwhelmingly won every battle in which he obeyed the Lord.

When others had seen only giants and defeat ... Joshua and Caleb had chosen to keep their eyes firmly set upon the strength and power of their God.

When others had fearfully exclaimed, "I can't!" Joshua declared, "God can!"

When others walked by sight ... Caleb walked by faith.

When others disobeyed ... Joshua obeyed.

When others ignored the voice of God ... Joshua and Caleb heard the voice of God.

When others turned tail and ran scared ... Joshua and Caleb followed the Lord with their whole heart.

The years passed quickly by and Caleb became an old man and

had yet another choice to make.

Would he retire or would he keep fighting with Joshua?

Would he put his feet up or would he and Joshua lead the people of God to greater victories?

Would he buy a condominium on the shores of the Jordan River or would he ask God for more?

What do you think that Caleb did? Consider the words of this man of faith:

"I was forty years old when Moses the servant of the Lord sent me to spy out the land, and I brought word back to him as it was in my heart.

Nevertheless my brethren who went up with me made the heart of the people melt with fear; but I followed the Lord my God fully.

So Moses wore on that day, saying 'Surely the land on which your foot has trodden will be an inheritance to you and to your children forever, because you have followed the Lord my God fully.'

"Now behold, the Lord has let me live, just as He spoke, these forty-five years, from the time that the Lord spoke this word to Moses, when Israel walked in the wilderness; and now behold, I am eighty-five years old today.

I am still as strong today as I was in the day Moses sent me; as my strength was then, so my strength is now, for war and for going out and coming in.

Now, then give me this hill country about which the Lord spoke on that day!"

—JOSHUA 14:7-12A

On Caleb's eighty-fifth birthday, he asked God for another mountain! Who does that?!

Caleb declared that his strength had not waned and that he had the courage for more battles ... more assignments ... more mountains ... more challenges ... new territory.

These days ... I often feel like Caleb did on his eighty-fifth birthday. I know that I have been assigned to take new territory for the Kingdom of God. I know that I will face giants in the land ... but when I consider the power of God ... the giants are like miniature fleas.

I know that I am not as young as I used to be ... but I am begging God to give me another mountain!

Where are you in life?

Are you asking God for another mountain? Or do you want riverfront property and a glass of iced tea? You see ... none of us can escape the call of Caleb.

Caleb's call is a call of power and of faith.

Caleb's life reminds you and me that one man ... or one woman ... when filled with the power of God ... truly can win battles too numerous to count!

What is the territory ... the mountain ... the enemy to whom you have been assigned?

Will you snore your way through life or will you wake up to the call and purposes of God?

I know that my God-ordained appointment is to make Hell smaller and Heaven bigger!

I know that my assigned territory is to conquer the giant of depression and usher in the promise of joy!

I know that the mountain of desperation is going down and that the promised land of "hope" will be a daily reality for women under my watch.

I know that prayers will be answered and that the voice of God will be heard ... *all because you and I answered the call of Joshua and Caleb at our moment in history.*

BIBLE READING

Hebrews 11

JOYFUL THOUGHTS TO PONDER

What was it that gave Joshua and Caleb the faith to know that they could indeed go into the Promised Land and conquer the giants?

How did Caleb have the strength to ask God for another mountain, a new assignment, even when he had lived a long time?

What is the mountain that you are asking God for today? Spend some time in prayer, either alone or with others, and ask God to give you that specific mountain!

Hebrews 11 is the "Hall of Fame" of men and women of faith. If the Holy Spirit were to write about your life, what would you want Him to say?

No Little Plans

It has always has seemed to me that in some unfortunate way the language of dreams, visions and setting goals are the fluent vernacular of only the very young. When I was a little girl, it was so easy to say what I wanted to do ... who I wanted to be ... what I wanted to accomplish ..."*when I grow up*".

I wanted to be a mommy and a teacher and a doctor and an astronaut and the first woman president.

I wanted to write books, to sing songs, to play piano for a symphony, to travel around the world and to make lots of money.

How heartbreakingly sad that we have minimized the ability to dream authentically and to plan with reckless abandon only to the very young at heart!

Whenever I return to my college alma mater and walk upon the acreage that houses the buildings of a world-class institution of higher learning, I am always challenged to dream again!

The sacred ground of my youth calls me once again to dream colossal dreams ... to embrace a stupendous vision ... and even to plan to move immense mountains!

Whenever I step upon that sacred piece of real estate that has been the launching pad for tens of thousands of alumni who have gone out into the world to serve God, I become a replica of my younger self. In those moments of touring a piece of my history, God stirs my heart to dream with the possibility of Heaven's involvement once again.

Going "home" to my university, has the precise effect on me as would traveling to that intangible mirage known as *"the fountain of youth"!*

As I walk up the stairs of the library, sit in a front-row seat at chapel and visit with the current students in my old dormitory, my heart is rejuvenated and my mind begins to imagine all of the possibilities of life that yet lie ahead of me. I am dreaming again!

Every time I return to this place of academic challenge, I am miraculously 20 years old again and I begin to speak easily and fluently the language of dreams and visions!

When I drive through the Avenue of Flags, my heart begins to beat rapidly and I initiate an internal inventory of *"Let's count your dreams! Let's take stock of future plans and visions!"*

The motto of our University is appropriately this quintuplet of words: *"Make no little plans here!"*

Those 5 powerful words are everywhere!!

They are on the desks of all of our professors.

"Make no little plans here!"

They are on T-shirts, coffee mugs and posters in the campus bookstore.

"Make no little plans here!"

They are on every 5-year, 10-year and 20-year plan that the University has ever conceived.

"Make no little plans here!"

Those 5 words are written on my heart and on the hearts of every one of the nearly 30,000 graduates:

"Make no little plans here!"

When was the last time that you returned to a place that forced you to dream again?

Regardless of your age, it is time for you to **dream again**!

Let each one of us ... old and young ... educated and uneducated ... purpose in our hearts to do something so grand and so humanly impossible that without the help of God, we will surely fail.

When Abram was weary with the constraints of age and saw no possibility of anything about his life ever changing, God took Abram outside to count the stars!

> *"And God took Abram outside and said, 'Now look toward the heavens, and count the stars, if you are able to count them.' And God said to Abram, 'So shall your descendants be.'"*

—GENESIS 15:5

God still loves to take His children outside of their pain, beyond their small thinking and past their weariness.

God still loves to confront each one of us with His vast plan and His infinite ability.

When God took Abram outside to play *"Let's Count the Stars!"*, Abram and God weren't actually looking at twinkling explosions of gaseous materials found light years away, but they were looking at the faces of all of the generations yet to come! They were gazing at the lives of men and women who would exist because Abram's tired, old seed was about to come in contact with the miraculous power of God!

When you play *"Let's Count the Stars!"* with God, what are **you** seeing?

Are you seeing books yet to be written and songs yet to be composed? Are you envisioning laws that need changing and orphans that need rescuing?

Do your stars in the vast sky of God represent businesses that will be built and degrees yet to be earned? Or, perhaps, like me, your stars are souls to be saved and missions trips to go on!

Will you take the time to go outside with God and count the stars of possibility with Him? I can tell you ... there is nothing like it!

He may just speak to you ... as He has to me ... *"Make no little plans here!"*

BIBLE READING

Genesis 15:1-7; Genesis 17:1-7

JOYFUL THOUGHTS TO PONDER

Why do you believe that it is easier for children to dream than it is for adults to dream?

Is it possible to "out-dream" God? Why or why not?

If you could accomplish one thing for the Kingdom of God, what would it be?

_____

_____

_____

Sing Louder!

The lyrics of songs ... of the great hymns of the faith ... and of contemporary worship have always touched my heart in deep and meaningful ways.

Words, when set to glorious melodies, become more than pedantic poetry; they become marching orders ... they become life-changing inspiration ... they become wisdom to live by ... and they become comfort to many a weary soul.

Vocabulary, when combined with music, has the tangible power of bringing life-changing impact and offering enthusiastic hope that soars.

Today, as I recover from yet another cancer surgery, let me share with you some of the lyrics that are stirring richly within my heart. Perhaps you would be interested in the "back-story" of these lyrics as well!

WE PRESS ON!

"When the valley is deep
When the mountain is steep
When the body is weary
When we stumble and fall

When the choices are hard
When we're battered and scarred

When we've spent our resources

When we've given our all

In Jesus' name, we press on

In Jesus' name, we press on

Dear Lord, with the prize clear before our eyes

We find the strength to press on."

Can anyone relate? Do I hear an "Amen!"?! Is there anyone reading who needs to be reminded to simply, *"Press On!"?!*

"We Press On", recorded by Selah, was written to a friend who was struggling in his faith. The words were meant to be an encouragement not to give up!

The lyrics were written with one obscure friend in mind and in heart. And yet, although written to one unknown person, these powerful words speak to you and to me that in spite of life's circumstances and in spite of unanswerable questions that we must keep our eyes firmly fixed on Jesus.

Done. I will press on. I will do it.

Or… how about these lyrics… written in 1882 by Louisa M. R. Stead?

'TIS SO SWEET TO TRUST IN JESUS!

"'Tis so sweet to trust in Jesus,

Just to take Him at His Word;

Just to rest upon His promise,

And to know, "Thus saith the Lord!"

Jesus, Jesus, how I trust Him!

How I've proved Him o'er and o'er;

Jesus, Jesus, precious Jesus!

Oh, for grace to trust Him more!

Yes, 'tis sweet to trust in Jesus,
Just from sin and self to cease;
Just from Jesus simply taking
Life and rest, and joy and peace.

Louisa Stead, the author of these tender lyrics, felt the call to missionary service from the time that she was just a little girl. However, ill health kept her from initially serving the Lord on foreign soil. She married young and had a daughter, Lily, whom she and her husband both completely adored.

When Lily was only 4 years old, the happy and Godly family of three decided to enjoy a sunny day at the beach at Long Island Sound. While eating their picnic lunch, they heard cries of, "Help! Help!" coming from the water. Louisa's husband went racing into the ocean to save a young boy who was drowning. As so often happens, the boy pulled his rescuer down with him and they both drowned while Louisa and Lily watched frantically from the shore.

What did Louisa do? What would you do if such a tragic event happened in your life?

Weep?! Wail with no control?! Blame?! Become Bitter?! Walk away from your faith and from your calling?

What Louisa did was that she wrote the lyrics to "'Tis So Sweet to Trust in Jesus!'"

Louisa knew the secret of singing through the fire. Rather than being scorched or maimed by the fire of tragedy, Louisa worshipped. The life of Louisa Stead lives on and on simply because she was a woman who decided to sing.

But perhaps the song that has played most loudly on the sound system of my heart over the course of 2015 is this one, written in 1903, by a man by the name of George Young:

GOD LEADS HIS DEAR CHILDREN ALONG

"In shady, green pastures, so rich and so sweet,
God leads His dear children along;

Where the water's cool flow bathes the weary one's feet,
God leads His dear children along.

Some through the waters, some through the flood,
Some through the fire, but all through the blood;
Some through great sorrow, but God gives a song,
In the night season and all the day long.

Sometimes on the mount where the sun shines so bright,
God leads His dear children along;
Sometimes in the valley, in darkest of night,
God leads His dear children along.

Though sorrows befall us and evils oppose,
God leads His dear children along;
Through grace we can conquer, defeat all our foes,
God leads His dear children along."

Who was this man by the name of George Young? Where did those powerful lyrics come from? Certainly he was a statesman ... or a renowned evangelist ... or a famous author.

Actually ... George Young was an obscure 19th Century preacher and carpenter who spent a lifetime humbly serving the Lord in small rural communities. Often his financial support was small, and life was hard on his family.

After a long struggle, the family was able to move into their own small home (which George built himself). However, when George was away preaching, some local thugs, who didn't like his Gospel preaching, set fire to the house, and it was totally destroyed.

It was out of that experience that Young reaffirmed his faith in God by writing God Leads His Dear Children Along.

But the story doesn't end with the song ...

Around 1942, a famous Christian hymnologist by the name of Dr.

Haldor Lillenas decided to track down George Young's widow and find out the story behind the lyrics as well as the story behind the man.

Lillenas was able to find an address in a small town and, driving there, he stopped at a gas station to ask for directions. When the attendant saw the address, he said, "Why sir, that's the County Poor House, up the road about three miles. And mister, when I say poor house, I really mean poor house!"

Not knowing what to expect, Lillenas made his way there. He found Mrs. Young, a tiny, elderly woman, in surroundings that were far from congenial. However, she radiated the joy of the Lord, and spoke of how the Lord had guided her and her husband over many years.

Then, the widow Young exclaimed, *"Dr. Lillenas, God led me here! I'm so glad He did, for you know, about every month someone comes into this place to spend the rest of their days...So many of them don't know my Jesus. I'm having the time of my life introducing them to Jesus! Dr. Lillenas, isn't it wonderful how God leads!"*

Read the defiant words to this resounding chorus one more time:

> *"Some through the waters, some through the flood,*
> *Some through the fire, but all through the blood;*
> *Some through great sorrow, but God gives a song,*
> *In the night season and all the day long!"*

Oh! We must linger in these words again!!

> *"Some through the waters, some through the flood,*
> *Some through the fire, but all through the blood;*
> *Some through great sorrow, but God gives a song,*
> *In the night season and all the day long!"*

I don't know what flood you are in today … but my advice to you is to keep on singing! Don't allow the roar of the ocean's waves to steal your song!

Sing louder than the flood!

I don't know what fire you are in today … but always remember that the blood of Jesus has the power to quench the fiery darts of any dastardly enemy crossfire!

Sing louder than the fire!

Even in the place of great human sorrow, God will give a song.

Sing louder than the sorrow!

Even in the darkest of all nights, the song of the Father pierces through the blackness and gives direction and hope.

Sing louder!

BIBLE READING

Psalm 3 & Psalm 4

JOYFUL THOUGHTS TO PONDER

What is your favorite hymn?

What is your favorite song to sing when you are weary or discouraged?

Why is music such a vital part of the Christian faith?

You might want to look up the story behind your favorite hymn! The history of the songs of our faith can actually enlarge the meaning of the lyrics.

_____

_____

_____

A Thousand Years!

I realized last night as I set my alarm, plumped my pillows for a final time, and turned out my bedside light, that I always dread the end of a day.

There is always an unspeakable sadness that washes over me at night as I lay my head down and pull the covers around my chin in the sweet moments before sleep overtakes me.

Another day has come and gone ... and this valuable day will never return to me.

I will never get to live this particular day again. This day has disappeared into the memory bank known as "the good old days" ... or "yesterday" ... or "the way we used to be".

This day has disappeared like the dew on the morning grass.

I now have one less day to live with passion in my heart and to enthusiastically embrace the life that I have been given with joy overflowing from every cell in my body.

One less day ...

I now have one less day of celebration ... of thanksgiving ... of gratitude ... of encouragement ... of hope ... of evangelism.

One less day ...

I now have one less day to pray healing prayers ... to share the Word ... to read my Bible ... to write a new book ... to change someone's life.

One less day ...

I now have one less day to hold a grandbaby ... to laugh with a daughter or daughter-in-law ... to have a rich conversation with a son or a son-in-law ... to call my mom and listen to her voice.

One less day ...

I now have one less day to love my husband ... to listen for God's compelling voice ... to reconnect with an old friend ... to visit somewhere that I have never been ... to worship this side of eternity.

One less day ...

I vividly recall other seasons of life when I couldn't WAIT to lay my head on the pillow! I couldn't WAIT to turn out the light and escape into a restful slumber. I couldn't WAIT for a day to finally be over!

But now is not that season. Now that unhurried symphony no longer plays on the strings of my heart.

Now there is a different melody playing: there is a fierce impatience in every measure and a rapidity of driving purpose wrapped in its very movement.

My life is not passing by in a pedantic march of boring procession but it is flying faster and faster in a rapid staccato of rhythm.

I feel like I am a little girl on a swiftly moving train as I watch the glory of life rush by and I am unable to catch it! I am unable to take a picture ... to embrace it ... to linger among the beauty of its days.

Oh! How I long for life to slow down!

Oh! How I deeply desire to thoroughly enjoy a day that moseys along with the languid movement of maple syrup fresh from the tree.

Why can't days dawdle like a little boy on his way to school?

Each day seems to be in a greater hurry than the last one and now I am incredulously left with much less time in front of me than I have behind me.

Life is pouring through the fingers of my heart without delay and I am unable to slowly cherish the treasure of each 24 hours that have been given to me.

I am out of breath watching my life scramble by with accelerating motion!

"Life! Slow down! I have just begun to live!"

"But do not let this one fact escape your notice, beloved, that with the Lord one day is like a thousand years and a thousand years like one day."

—II PETER 3:8

And when I read the ancient words ... the sacred words ... that have lived in the heart of God for all of eternity ... my heart begins to rest. Peace comes flooding into my human soul and replaces the panic that has momentarily taken up residence in my heart.

The Lord does indeed have a perspective on time and eternity that is a balm to my out-of-breath existence and He calls me *"Beloved"* as He speaks.

Just hearing His voice whisper, *"Beloved"* replaces my panic with His purpose.

Peter and the Holy Spirit gently remind me, the *"Beloved"*, that the way that God views time and the way that I view time are light years apart.

From God's perspective, He can place one thousand years of purpose into one ordinary day! If I have 25 years of life left ... that is 9,150 days in my calendar book but to God ... it has the impact of 9,150,000 years!

I adore the way that God views time! I need His eternal perspective so much more than I need my temporary melancholy melody!

God is able to take a 24-hour period of time and pack so much purpose, delight and abundance into it that it takes on the weight and meaning of a thousand years of living! How is that for mathematics?!

And so tonight when I lay my weary head on the pillow, I will not have a tear dripping down my wrinkled cheek, but I will smile as I look ahead to the one thousand years of living that God and I intend to embrace over the next 24 hour period!

BIBLE READING

Psalm 6 and Psalm 7

JOYFUL THOUGHTS TO PONDER

Do you dread the end of a day or are you grateful to lay your head on your pillow at night? What determines that difference?

What is your interpretation of II Peter 3:8? Do you have any insight into that verse?

How does viewing your life from an eternal perspective make a difference in how you also view the passing of time?

What is an "eternal perspective"? What does that mean to you?

_____

_____

_____

A Toothpick of a Boy

David and Goliath.

Insurmountable mountains. Unwinnable battles. Unbeatable odds.

What do you do when life is stacked up against you? What do you do when there seems to be no way out of the wilderness ... no favorable outcome in the making ... no hope of survival?

What do you do?

I think that you do what David did ... you begin to declare the victorious power of God!

You walk toward your giant with no fear but with the grandest faith in the greatest of Gods!

Are you facing a giant today? Have you more than met your match in the circumstances of life that have piled up around you into a mountain of impossibility?

If so ... you might want to read on.

David was just a little shepherd boy who often wrote songs in the middle of the night. He was the youngest of a whole bunch of brothers and often may have felt overlooked or underappreciated. Perhaps it was hard for him to figure out his identity in the family of Jesse. I wonder ...

David's three older brothers had enlisted in the army of Saul. David not only had to tend the family flock in his brothers' absence but he also had to go back and forth between the family farm and the battlegrounds in order to take food to his brothers.

One day, as young David was approaching the place where the army was encamped, a giant of a man began to taunt the army of Saul. This colossal enemy with his resounding voice and pounding footsteps fiercely intimidated the entire army of Israel. David's older brothers, along with the rest of the army, fled! They ran scared in the opposite direction of Goliath with dry mouths and with pounding hearts.

Their very lives were on the line. This was a man who could do great damage to anyone and anything in his pathway.

The gargantuan Goliath. The Hulk. A monster of a man. Was he a man or was he a beast?!

When David encountered the terror-stricken men of Israel's finest, all David could do was talk about killing this giant!

> *"Then David spoke to the men who were standing by him, saying, 'What will be done for the man who kills this Philistine and takes away the reproach from Israel? For who is this uncircumcised Philistine, that he should taunt the armies of the living God?!'"*

> —I SAMUEL 17:26

Who *IS* this Philistine?!

What *IS* your battle?!

Why *IS* that mountain in your way?!

Following David's incredulous questioning, David's brothers became undone with him. They were angry at this little piece of a boy and considered him to be a willful and annoying brat.

> *"Now Eliab his oldest brother heard when he spoke to the men; and Eliab's anger burned against David and he said, 'Why have you come down? And with whom have you left those few sheep in the wilderness? I know your insolence and the wickedness of your heart; for you have come down in order to see the battle.'"*

> —I SAMUEL 17:28

What have you been accused of?

Have people mocked you for your faith ... for your hope ...

for your joy?!

Is it difficult to find people who stand with you in the challenges of life?

Although young and inexperienced with giants, David had prepared for this epic moment. He was no stranger to fighting with that which was fierce and able to kill with one vicious roar ... with one tiny bite ... with one sharp claw.

> *"But David said to Saul, 'Your servant was tending his father's sheep. When a lion or a bear came and took a lamb from the flock, I went out after him and attacked him, and rescued it from his mouth; and when he rose up against me, I seized him by his beard and struck him and killed him. Your servant has killed both the lion and the bear; and this uncircumcised Philistine will be like one of them, since he has taunted the armies of the living God.'"*

> —I SAMUEL 17:34-36

Nothing scared this toothpick of a boy! He was already an expert in tearing apart ravenous lions and in mutilating marauding bears. Why should a hulking giant who did not have the Lord on his side threaten David? Why indeed?!

What have you done to prepare for the giants in life?

Have you run away in fear or have you fought to the finish?!

I have another question for you today ...

What do you talk about when confronted with an insurmountable mountain ... with an unwinnable battle ... or by unbeatable odds?

What do you talk about?!

David couldn't stop talking about God! His focus wasn't on the giant ... His focus was on the God Who was infinitely superior to a little old giant!

David wasn't trash-talking ... He was triumphantly declaring the power and the authority of His Lord!

> *And David said, 'The Lord who delivered me from the paw of*
> *the lion and from the paw of the bear, He will deliver me from the*
> *hand of this Philistine.' And Saul said to David, 'Go, and may the*
> *Lord be with you.'"*

—I SAMUEL 17:37

What you choose to talk about at the most frightening and traumatic moment of your life reveals what is in your heart. Are you more aware of the presence and power of God or of the unfairness and alarm of your circumstances?

Oh to be like little David! I long to be a woman who thinks about … talks about … is focused on … the overwhelming and majestic greatness of the God Whom I serve.

Oh to understand in every battle that I face that the battle is not mine to lose but it is the Lord's to win!

> *"Then David said to the Philistine, 'You come to me with a sword,*
> *a spear and a javelin, but I come to you in the name of the Lord of*
> *hosts, the God of the armies of Israel, whom you have taunted. This*
> *day the Lord will deliver you up into my hands and I will strike*
> *you down and remove your head from you. And I will give the dead*
> *bodies of the army of the Philistines this day to the birds of the sky*
> *and the wild beasts of the earth, that all the earth may know that*
> *there is a God in Israel."*

—I SAMUEL 17:45 – 46

Stop talking **about** your mountain and start talking **to** your mountain! Stop talking **about** the enormous size of your giant and start **telling** your giant exactly what he is going to look like when God is done with him!

Start declaring the glory and power of God over every battle that you face!

Let's take the words "insurmountable" … "unwinnable" … and "unbeatable" out of our vocabulary and replace them with the words "triumphant" … "victorious" … and "more than a conqueror"!

Let's believe that God is Who He says He is and that He can do what He says He can do! Let's join David ... that little toothpick of a boy ... and face the giants who dare interrupt our lives! Let's defeat behemoth giants and move towering mountains and win relentless battles with the extraordinary strength that comes from Heaven and with the declaration of God's presence and power.

BIBLE READING

I Samuel 17

JOYFUL THOUGHTS TO PONDER

What are some of the giants that you have faced in your life? Have your giants conquered you or have you conquered them?

Why does it matter how we talk about our giants?

Was David's focus on Goliath or on God? Why does it matter what we focus on?

What lesson do you believe that his brothers and the army of Israel learned from David? What lessons have you learned from David?

_____

_____

_____

When Hope Is Your Only Hope

What do you do when the bottom has dropped out?

Why ... you hold onto hope, of course!

What do you do when the most ferocious of storms is threatening all that you value and all that is dear in life?

Why ... you tie yourself to the anchor of hope, of course!

What do you do when mountains won't move and when deserts are hot and when people walk away?

What in the world do you do?

My advice to you is to find a single strand of hope ... to tie it to your heart ... and then refuse to let it slip away.

Sometimes ... hope is your only hope.

Hope is one of the greatest gifts and most valuable treasures in a human life. A serious problem presents itself when we are more aware of our disappointment and heart pain than we are of hope.

But what exactly is this diamond called "hope"? And where in the world do you find it?

Can hope be bought or sold?

It's been my experience that although hope is not found in any store or at any online venue, you do possess something that you are able to trade in order to become the proud owner of "hope".

It is possible, indeed, to exchange your disappointment and pain for an astounding sliver of hope. The amazing truth is this ... all it takes is a sliver of hope. Just the tiniest sliver of hope is able to add great value to a disintegrating life.

Isn't that astounding?! You take your pain to the Father ... and He gives you hope!

Just a sweet reminder, though ... you will never receive hope while you are holding onto discouragement and heart pain. Hope and disappointment are mutually exclusive. It is impossible for "hope" and "disappointment" to exist in the same heart.

You can gather up all of your discouragement ... your frustration ... your envy ... and your disappointment ... and throw it at the throne of God Almighty! And do you know what he gently yet powerfully gives you in return?

He presents to you the hope of Sarah and Abraham before your circumstances ever change!

> *"Even as Abraham believed God and it was accounted to him for righteousness."*
>
> —GALATIANS 3:6

> *"By faith, even Sarah herself received ability to conceive, even beyond the proper time of life, since she considered Him faithful who had promised."*
>
> —HEBREWS 11:11

He bequeaths the hope of Joshua to a battle-weary soul.

> *"By faith, the walls of Jericho fell down after they had been encircled for seven days."*
>
> —HEBREWS 11:30

When all you see are impossibilities and certain destruction, our God is well able to endow the hope and faith of Moses.

> *"By faith, Moses, when he had grown up, refused to be called the*

son of Pharaoh's daughter, choosing rather to endure ill-treatment with the people of God than to enjoy the passing pleasures of sin."

—HEBREWS 11:24 & 25

"By faith, they passed through the Red Sea as though they were passing through dry land and the Egyptians, when they attempted it, were drowned."

—HEBREWS 11:29

When the winds wail and the storms crash around the little boat of your life, God will give to you the anchor of His hope.

"So that by two unchangeable things in which it is impossible for God to lie, we who have taken refuge would have strong encouragement to take hold of the hope set before us. This hope we have as an anchor of the soul, a hope both sure and steadfast..."

—HEBREWS 6:18 & 19

Hope is tenacious and bold and stubborn. Hope outlasts ... out shouts ... and outsings any human emotion of the soul.

Hope is not an emotion nor is it a mere strength of human personality. Hope finds its conception in the very heart of Christ.

You will never have true hope until you have Christ.

The world often will present counterfeits of this eternal substance known as "hope". The culture in which you live will try to convince you that positive thinking is enough ... that pulling yourself up by your bootstraps is enough ... that it is simply time for you to put on your big girl panties and get a grip.

Frankly ... none of those humanistic philosophies have ever worked for me and I have tried them all.

I doubt that they will work for you, either.

There is only one eternal tenet that regulates my heartbeat when times are tough and when life is devastating. There is one only one.

Hope.

Hope is the full assurance that God is in control. Hope is the God-given guarantee that I am not nor will I ever be forgotten.

Hope is the joy of His presence ... it is the peace that rushes in as a result of trusting the good Father ... and it delivers the wisdom of the ages.

Hope is more than enough strength ... it is more than enough power ... and it is more than enough promise to shield me from any category 5 storm in life!

Hope, although it often whispers, is louder than my craziest fears and is the most vibrant and active cheerleader in my life.

Hope has the expertise to dig into the manure of my heart and to replace the rotting issues with the sweet and fragrant promise of Spring.

If your life is a mass of confusion, pain and disappointment, know that God wants to envelop your soul with His hope. Hope is only found in Him. There is no other source of hope.

Hope is not found in a candidate, in a destination, in a degree plan or in a marriage license.

Hope cannot be discovered in pay raises or bonuses, in real estate acquisitions or in career promotions.

> *"Are there any among the idols of the nations who give rain? Or can the heavens grant showers? Is it not You, O Lord our God? Therefore, we hope in You, for You are the One who has done all these things."*
>
> —JEREMIAH 14:22

Hope happens when I join my heart with His in a glorious symphony of praise to His faithfulness and unconditional love.

> *"Why are you in despair, O my soul? And why have you become disturbed within me? Hope in God, for I shall yet praise Him, the help of my countenance and my God."*
>
> —PSALM 42:11

BIBLE READING
Psalm 42

JOYFUL THOUGHTS TO PONDER
Define the word "hope".

What are you hoping for currently in your life?

How can you connect your deepest hopes to your prayer life?

How does hope differ from faith?

_____

_____

_____

Turn Up the Volume!

I am expecting God to speak to me.

Are you expecting God to speak to you?

I am confidently expecting God to speak to me.

Are you? Are you confidently expecting God to speak to you?

Whenever I enter into an attitude of child-like anticipation that God is about to speak to me ... an ordinary girl ... it is in that moment of expectation that everything I experience becomes a possible missive from Heaven.

A sermon becomes the voice of God.

A worship song is a telegram from Heaven.

A daily devotional becomes a special delivery letter with my name on it.

Today, I am confidently expecting God to speak to me.

And then ... I wonder why I don't *always* approach life with the same anticipation. What is it about today that makes it any different than yesterday or than last week?

Why don't I approach every day with the desperate desire to hear from the heart of God?

I have no answer for that question ... but this is what I do know:

God wants to speak to His children more than we desire to listen.

How do I know that ? Well, I know that because I am a mom with 5 adult children. I long to have a heart to heart conversation with each one of my children every day. But that rarely happens.

The reason that speaking with my children daily happens so infrequently is because they are busy living productive and powerful lives. I don't want to interrupt their daily commitments and appointments and so I wait for them to call me.

And when they do call me ... I can tell. I can tell immediately whether the conversation will be 2 minutes in length or will be a leisurely time of enjoying the sound of one another's voices.

I can tell whether this particular conversation will be a rushed exchange of, "Just the facts, ma'm. Only the facts."

Or if the long desired conversation will be a time of volleying back and forth ... of listening ... of crying and laughing.

How I long for the latter ... but I will settle for the former.

I will settle for the former because I am the mom and any exchange of words and information is a comfort to me.

But, oh how I long for the latter!

I long for an uninterrupted consultation of prayer requests, sweet stories and heart to heart sharing.

That is what a parent's heart always longs for.

We ache to talk to our kids day or night.

Early or late.

Convenient or inconvenient.

Long or short.

It doesn't matter with whom I am having lunch ... what deadline I am facing ... or how involved I am in any important project ... when I see one of my kids' names on my cell phone ... everything else is instantly dropped and sometimes forgotten.

I have a feeling that God, the Father, responds much the same ways as Carol, the mother does.

He aches to speak with us. He aches to listen to us.

And He is waiting lovingly for our call.

Now ... another aspect of a vital and life-giving conversation is which participant does the talking and which participant does the listening?

If one person does all the talking without taking a breath it is not actually a conversation. It is a soliloquy. It is a monologue.

It is one-sided. It is selfish. It is boring.

A healthy conversation always contains give and take ... words and silence ... questions and answers ... conundrums and advice.

Do you know what this mother's heart does when one of my children say, "Mom ... I called to get some advice. What do you think?"

Do you know the absolute joy in this mother's heart when one of my children actually asks for and then leans into my advice and counsel?

Touché.

'Nuff said.

I hope that you "get" the correlation. It's rather obvious.

The heart of God is waiting for your phone call. He does indeed have some wisdom to speak into your life. He is aching for you to begin the conversation.

God has input ... and advice ... and knowledge ... and perspective ... that you need more than you realize. But like a distracted child, you remain immersed in self-appointed productivity ... and meetings ... and busyness ... and horizontal conversations.

He longs to speak with you and to you ... is it your desperate need to listen to Him today?

I have an audacious desire to hear the voice of God and I will set aside every distraction, every deceptive priority and every earthly interference in order to hear from Heaven.

Speak Lord, Your servant is listening.

BIBLE READING

I Samuel 3

JOYFUL THOUGHTS TO PONDER

How do you hear the voice of God? Through what venue or method does God often speak to you?

Is God still speaking today or did He stop speaking when the Bible was completed?

Make a list of all of the ways that you could potentially hear the voice and heart of God.

_____

_____

_____

Commonly Uncommon

I have always wanted to be an incredible person. Does that sound prideful to you? I truly don't mean it to be presumptuous or pretentious in nature ... just honest.

I have always deeply desired to live an amazing and unforgettable life of great passion and of relentless enthusiasm.

I have wanted my life to smack of Heaven's participation and to be a grand show and tell of joyful and surprising miracles!

I have never wanted to settle for mundane ... or for mediocre ... or for average.

> *"Ho! Everyone who thirsts, come to the waters;*
>
> *And you who have no money come, buy and eat.*
>
> *Come, buy wine and milk without money and without cost."*
>
> —ISAIAH 55:1

I have yearned that the words "Carol" and "common" would never be used in the same sentence. I have wished that those two words would be mutually exclusive in meaning and in content.

> *"Why do you spend money for what is not bread,*
>
> *and your wages for what does not satisfy?*
>
> *Listen carefully to Me, and eat what is good,*
>
> *And delight yourself in abundance!"*
>
> —ISAIAH 55:2

Now ... looking at my life from the outside ... you might assume that much of my life is just that. It might seem from your perspective that I have settled for mundane ... or for mediocre ... or for average. You might falsely believe that "Common Carol" is the moniker attached to my existence.

But nothing could be further from the truth!

> *"Incline your ear and come to Me.*
>
> *Listen, that you may live;*
>
> *And I will make an everlasting covenant with you,*
>
> *According to the faithful mercies shown to David."*
>
> —ISAIAH 55:3

You see ... I am more aware of ordinary miracles than I am of my own existence. I am absolutely smitten by the wonder of creation ... by the whimsy of a beautiful poem ... and by the sound of the laughter of children.

I can't get enough of autumn leaves ... and of Spring flowers bursting forth ... and of sweetly drifting snowflakes ... and of the sound of bumblebees and birds!

My heart pounds in enthusiastic anticipation of what the next day holds ... of what the next week will bring ... and of what the next hour will deliver to my front door!

> *"Seek the Lord while He may be found;*
>
> *Call upon Him while He is near."*
>
> —ISAIAH 55:6

Although just like you, I get up every day and brush my teeth, make my messy bed and fold yet another load of unending laundry, still every breath that I breathe sparkles with the hope of an unexpected blessing and with the priceless gift of yet another friend.

I tremble when I realize that I, just an ordinary girl, have the capacity to reveal the heart and love of Christ as I slog through this journey called "life".

What is common about that?!

"Let the wicked forsake His way and the unrighteous man his thoughts;

And let him return to the Lord,

And He will have compassion on him;

And to our God, for He will abundantly pardon."

—ISAIAH 55:7

I serve a God who forgave me so that I could live a life of smashing possibility and of exponential faith! He didn't forgive me so that I would listlessly just "make it" through another boring day ... but He forgave me abundantly so that I could sing my way through sorrow and hope my way through discouragement!

Now that's the life that I am talking about!

"For my thoughts are not your thoughts,

nor are your ways My ways," declares the Lord.

For as the heavens are higher than the earth,

So are my ways higher than your ways

and My thoughts than your thoughts."

—ISAIAH 55:8 & 9

God has created a life so grand for me that I can't begin to tap into it with my human thinking patterns. I must discover a way to think like God ... emote like God ... love like God ... dream like God ... hope like God ... believe like God! Is that even possible?!

"For as the rain and snow come down from Heaven,

And do not return there without watering the earth

And making it bare and sprout,

And furnishing seed to the sower and bread to the eater;

So will My Word be which goes forth from My mouth;

It will not return to Me empty,

Without accomplishing what I desire,

And without succeeding in the matter for which I sent it."

—ISAIAH 55:10 & 11

God's Word will enable me to live a life of Heaven's grandeur and of daily miracles! God's Word is on assignment in my life to accomplish great things for all of eternity! Are you speechless yet? Are you breathless with the anticipation of what you were designed to accomplish in partnership with God's Word?!

You were not made for ordinary! You were made for eternity ... and for miracles ... and for thinking like God ... and to live an incredible life in a human body!

"For you will go out with joy!

And be led forth with peace!

The mountains and the hills will break forth into shouts of joy before you!

And all the trees of the field with clap their hands!"

—ISAIAH 55:12

Often, people don't understand me. They don't understand or even agree with my commitment to joy. Often, people whose lives have collapsed in a pile of tragedy, unending injustice and complete mediocrity, don't want to be confronted with the possibility of living a life of joy.

And that's OK ... they get to live their life the way they choose to do so ... and I will live my life in the manner that I deem best for me.

And for me ... the Word of God has miraculously changed me from depressed to joyful. His Word did indeed accomplish the purpose for which it was sent from Heaven to little ole' me.

And for me ... I have embraced a peace that passes understanding. I don't always like my circumstances nor would I always choose them

… but my circumstances don't determine my level of peace. I serve the Prince of Peace who guarantees peace. That's good enough for me.

And that incredible person that I have always wanted to be?! The mountains and the hills of His creation are giving me a standing. Oh my name may not be written in any history book … but God's creation has taken note of my extraordinary ordinary life and is roaring with approval!

BIBLE READING

Isaiah 55

JOYFUL THOUGHTS TO PONDER

What are some of the dreams and goals you had as a child?

What is the greatest miracle that you have ever seen in your life?

If you could change one thing about your life today, what would it be? How can you partner with God to change this thing?

_____

_____

_____

Thanksgiving ... Thanks-speaking ... Thanks-singing ... Thanks-living!

What sweet memories I have of Thanksgiving days gone by! The rich and precious treasure of the Thanksgivings of yesterday invariably will cause the tears to flow in abundance ... my heart to swell with a quiet aching ... and my gaze to lift Heavenward.

The crackle of the fire in the blazing and inviting fireplace.

My mother's white linen tablecloth spread on the seldom-used dining room table.

The smell of the turkey roasting in the oven.

Pumpkin pies cooling on the countertop.

My grandmother's tart but delectably sweet cranberry recipe.

Family gathered from far and near. Tulsa. Nashville. Pennsylvania. Texas. New York City. India.

Missing deeply those who are unable to join us around the table.

It's the thankful time of year.

Thanksgiving is truly one of my favorite holidays. I love the seasonal reminder that there is so much that I have been given to which thankfulness is the appropriate and necessary response.

I delight in the knowledge that people across the nation pause for a rare moment in time and remember to speak forth words of heartfelt gratitude.

Thanksgiving is a time for remembering ... for being grateful ... for resting in all that He is and all that He has done.

I don't know what your Thanksgiving table will look like this year ... or who will be gathered around it. But I want to barge myself uninvited into your annual celebration of gratitude and share with you a few things that God has been sharing with me.

So ... from God's heart ... to my heart ... to your Thanksgiving table ...

Thanksgiving is not a single day on the calendar but it was always meant to be a lifestyle. Thanksgiving is the particular way that we are able to access the presence of the Father.

> *"Enter His gates with thanksgiving and His courts with praise."*
>
> —PSALM 100:4

Thanksgiving was never meant to be an annual celebration identified by pilgrims, pies and stuffing ... but it was meant to be the most accurate demonstration of relationship between children and their heavenly, generous Father. As the family of God, we are called to respond daily ... hourly ... moment by moment ... as the beneficiaries of the miraculous blessings given from Heaven's resources to our wilderness table of life.

The only possible response is, "Thanks, Dad!"

And we must not wait for a month or a day on a calendar to provoke this heartfelt thanksgiving! We are compelled to shout it out continually because we are simply quite unable to hold it back.

> *"Enter with the password: "Thank You!" Make yourselves at home, talking praise. Thank Him. Worship Him."*
>
> —PSALM 100:4— *THE MESSAGE BIBLE*

Thanks-speaking is the language of the family of the Father. It is our native tongue. We don't speak with words of complaining ... in the tongue of lack ... or with the accent of griping. We are thanks-speakers every day of every year. We have learned this particular language at the knee of the Father.

Words of rich gratitude fill the dictionary of our hearts and from its deep treasuries we write the story of our lives.

I am thankful for my home, family and job.

I am grateful for food, for heat, for a car.

Thanks, Dad, for my church family and for my crazy family! I love them both!

Father, thank you for coffee ... and for the giggle of a baby ... and for the local library.

I am so thankful for friends who make me laugh ... keep me humble ... and challenge my thinking processes.

I am grateful for people who enable me to respond like You would.

I am thankful for snow and for sunshine ... for thunderstorms ... and for Spring days.

I am thankful for my Bible ... for worship music ... for prayers both answered and unanswered ... and for YOU, my Father!

Thanks-singing is the choice that has the joyful ability to turn the dry and barren wilderness into a fruitful and lush garden of life.

If you choose to wait to sing until you "feel" like singing ... you may never sing again! Feelings don't determine the frequency of our song ... the depth of the harmonies ... or the breadth of its audience.

The song that fills the days of our lives is birthed in the heart of the Father's love for us. He loves me! That gives me something to sing about every day of every year!

When the arctic winds of January are wailing ... God gives a song!

When February 14th comes around again and relationships remain difficult and demanding ... or your heart shivers from perpetual loneliness ... He sings a love song into personal darkness and pain.

When the Winter stubbornly lingers into March and April ... He sings of His vibrant power and we join bravely in the duet with Him.

And then ... when at last Spring flowers bloom and the warmth of sunshine re-appears ... the song delightfully grows in volume not because of human happiness but because of His dear presence.

And when the flowers fade ... and the leaves begin to fall ... and the earth prepares itself for Winter's ferocious onslaught ... the song remains steady and strong as the children of God sing with the saints of the ages,

> *"Great is Thy Faithfulness! O God, my Father!*
> *There is no shadow of turning with Thee!*
> *Thou changest not, Thy compassions they fail not.*
> *Great is Thy Faithfulness, Lord unto me!"*

Thanks-living is what life is all about! The only reason that you and I are still alive this year is to give Him more thanks ... higher praise ... and louder worship.

We do not live for selfish ambition or for personal gain but we live to worship Him!

We breathe to sing to Him!

We exist to write a new song of wondrous thanksgiving and glorious worship!

Our lives are the song that He has been aching to hear this year. Like a proud papa, He is bending low to hear our childlike attempts at singing a new and challenging song.

Frankly, the Father doesn't care if we are on pitch or off pitch ... He doesn't notice whether we hit the right notes or the painful, wrong ones ... He is not concerned with perfection or performance. The Father just wants to hear the song.

And so ... when you sit down at the Thanksgiving table this year to indulge in the laughter of family, the bounty of provision and the delight of memories ... don't forget why you were created! You are alive today in order to sing the song that the pilgrims of faith sang with gusto and with wholehearted joy! You are here to join in the symphony of praise of those who have gone before but who have served with thanksgiving at their moment in eternity's calendar.

> *We gather together to ask the Lord's blessing;*
> *He chastens and hastens His will to make known;*
> *The wicked oppressing now cease from distressing;*

Sing praises to His Name; He forgets not His own.

Beside us to guide us, our God with us joining,
Ordaining, maintaining His kingdom divine;
So from the beginning the fight we were winning;
Thou, Lord, were at our side, all glory be Thine!

We all do extol Thee, Thou Leader triumphant,
And pray that Thou still our Defender will be;
Let Thy congregation escape tribulation;
Thy Name be ever praised! O Lord, make us free!

BIBLE READING
Psalm 100 and Psalm 65:9-13

JOYFUL THOUGHTS TO PONDER
What are your favorite memories of Thanksgiving?

Write out a simple definition of these four words:

Thanksgiving

Thanks-speaking

Thanks-singing

Thanks-living

Which one are you most successful at? Which one do you struggle with the most?

_____

_____

_____

What Can I Give Him?

The songs of Christmas pronounce the very meaning, the genuine heart and the vivid story of this holy season. The carols that have grown so vibrant throughout the decades embrace the heartfelt message of Christmas in every stanza … in every melody … and in every word.

More than the food of holiday parties, the songs of this season fill all of the ravenous places in humanity.

More than the lights on every home on every street, the hymns of Christmas light up the darkness with His presence.

More than the mountain of gifts under the family Christmas tree, the joyful and hopeful anthems of advent give generously to a world awash with expectation.

"A thrill of hope the weary world rejoices!"

Into our weariness came a Savior. The tired travelers of life are now rejoicing because of hope. Simply because of the song that only hope sings. Do you hear the song of hope? Is hope singing in your world today?

"Mary, did you know that your Baby Boy has walked where angels trod?

When you kiss your little Baby you kissed the face of God?"

Mary … the virgin who was no more than a girl herself … kissed the face of God. Oh to be there that night when the angels sang and the shepherds danced! Oh to watch this young mother fall in love with Heaven's darling!

"Hallelujah! Oh, how the angels sang! Hallelujah! How it rang!

And the sky was bright with a holy light! 'Twas the birthday of a King!"

His birthday was a night when the darkness of a world in pain exploded with rare and glorious colors! That night that Jesus was born was a night when the voices of an angelic choir roared in victory! That night!

"Oh come to my heart, Lord Jesus, there is room in my heart for Thee."

I am my own innkeeper ... and I must decide if there is room for Him or not. Will I cast away other interests and distractions in order to make a place in my heart for Him? Or does my heart embarrassingly declare, "No Vacancy"?

And we dare not overlook this triumphant theological treatise that fills the canyons of our frightened world with joy explosive!

"Hail the Heaven born Prince of Peace! Hail the Son of Righteousness!

Light and life to all He brings, Risen with healing in His wings.

Mild He lays His glory by, Born that man no more may die;

Born to raise the sons of earth, Born to give them second birth;

Hark! The herald angels sing, "Glory to the newborn King!"

Jesus, the Son of the Most High God, left the glory of Heaven so that you and I would not have to experience the pains of death! He was born so that we could be born again! No wonder the angels sang!

My heart joins in the Christmas anthem that resounds through eternity! I can't stop singing the melodies ... the lyrics ... and the hymns that declare Christmas!

But perhaps it is the songs that children sing during this holy season that speak the loudest and linger the longest.

"Be near me, Lord Jesus, I ask Thee to stay

Close by me forever and love me I pray.

Bless all the dear children in Thy tender care,

And take us to Heaven to live with Thee there."

Oh to experience the faith and joy of a child at Christmas time! To know that Jesus came for me and that His love is truly the only gift that matters!

"Sleep well, little children, pleasant dreams through the night;

Tomorrow is Christmas, all merry and bright.

Soon you'll hear the bells ring, time for dreams to come true;

As the world wakes to bring, Merry Christmas to you."

One of the greatest miracles of Christmas is that the entire world joins in the proclamation! Christmas has a singular and dynamic song that cannot be stilled and will not be silent. Christmas awakens each one of our hearts to hope ... to joy ... and to the Light of the World.

"I played my drum for Him pa-rum pum pum pum

I played my best for Him pa-rum pum pum pum

Rum pum pum pum, rum pum pum pum

Then He smiled at me pa-rum pum pum pum

Me and my drum."

The Christ child of Christmas smiles at the child in all of us when we sing for Him. Your song may not be the loudest song or the strongest song ... but sing anyway! Sing at the top of your lungs and from deep within your heart this year at Christmas!

Don't let the pain of the past year silence your song or stifle your joy. The song of Christmas is a song that resounds over the mountains and the valleys of life. The anthem of this season echoes triumphantly over human pain and in spite of deep disappointment.

The joyous carols of Christmas have the intensity that it takes to boil away the distractions of the season and then to help us to focus anew on why He came. He came for you ... He came for me.

That's what Christmas is all about. He came.

He came so that we could sing.

He came so that we could hope.

He came so that we could live.

My deepest prayer is that when you sing the songs of Christmas this year that you will be reminded of the matchless and glorious miracle of Christmas. This Baby ... the little Boy in the manger ... changed everything for you and for me.

What can I give Him poor as I am?

If I were a shepherd, I would bring Him a Lamb

If I were a wise man, I'd sure do my part

So what can I give Him? I'll give Him my heart

I'll give Him my heart, Give Him my heart

What can I can give Him but all of my heart?

I'll give Him my heart, Give Him my heart

What can I give Him but all of my heart?

What can you give Him? What can you bring?

What can you offer that's fit for a King?

Bow before Jesus that's where you can start

What can you give Him? Just Give Him your heart

Give Him your heart! Give Him your heart!

What can you give Him but all of your heart?

Give Him your heart! Give Him your heart!

What can you give Him? Just give Him your heart

BIBLE READING

Luke 1:1-38

JOYFUL THOUGHTS TO PONDER

What is your favorite hymn or song of the Christmas season?

How does it honor Christ when we sing for Him and to Him?

Can you think of some instances in the Christmas story in the Bible when music or songs were part of the announcement?

Make plans to attend a Christmas concert at a school or at a church this Christmas season.

_____

_____

_____

The Best of Times ... The Worst of Times

"It was the best of times ... it was the worst of times ..." are the unforgettable words that begin "A Tale of Two Cities" written by Charles Dickens who also famously penned "A Christmas Carol".

"It was the best of times ... it was the worst of times ..." are also, unfortunately, the words that many of us have used to emotionally and spiritually pen our Christmas stories and memories.

"It was the best of times ..." are the 6 words jubilantly chosen to describe a holiday cup that is frothy and running over with cheer, gifts, healthy relationships and a beautifully decorated home.

"It was the best of times ..." seems to be the caption that is used to describe an iconic Rockwellian picture of a snow-decked landscape looking into the window of a red and green home that has an interesting yet functional family at its core. The kids are throwing wrapping paper everywhere ... the parents are still dressed in their robes with deep circles under their eyes yet are able to smile at the noise and confusion ... the holiday turkey is browning perfectly in the oven with its aroma wafting through the expectant air ... and Granma is on her way with a sleigh filled with pumpkin pies and figgy pudding!

It certainly IS the best of times!

"It was the worst of times" ... are often the December lyrics of choice when the bottom has fallen out of one's shaky attempt at living.

Food stamps may be a daily reality and necessity.

The dysfunction of family relationships may be a constant

reminder of what is most wrong with life.

This Christmas may be spent in the terror of the ICU rather than by the warmth of a welcoming fireplace with eggnog in one hand and a Christmas cookie in the other.

Perhaps rather than torturous relationships to deal with, there is no family to gather around the sparsely bedecked caricature of Charlie Brown's famous tree.

Your money perhaps is scarce and your health, at best, is questionable. Perhaps you are just one mortgage payment away from losing the family home and because of that there will be no Santa Claus coming down the chimney this year to leave a memorable deposit of materialism under the lonely tree.

Christmas can often be, truly, *the worst of times.*

However, I happen to believe, that judging the authenticity or joy of Christmas by what we have or do not have is a foolish and impulsive mistake of gargantuan and even eternal proportions.

Christmas was never meant to be measured by human standards or by a glass that is gleefully half-full or agonizingly half-empty.

What one sees circumstantially is largely unable to coincide with earth's attempt at fulfillment because of Heaven's promise of delivered joy!

See ... it is not in what you do have or do not have that should determine how you are able to describe your Christmas this year or any calendar year! It is always found ... eternally found ... in Who He is!

He is joy when your life seems empty.

He is peace when all around you are in conflict.

He is hope when all human wells have run dry.

He is the Healer in a life that is sick, fragile and wasted.

He is Christmas!

He is what makes any day of any year *the very best of times.*

Don't be so small in your expectations of a truly memorable Christmas that you boil it down to gifts, a bevy of celebratory people or how much red and green is strewn around your home.

Instead, this Christmas, remember what Christmastime is powerfully all about:

A young woman who has had her world invaded with the promise that with God ... all things are possible!

The plans of a young man that were hurriedly changed because the God of the universe interrupted his human desire for happy ever after.

A manure-filled, mouse-scurrying stable that welcomed the Baby who was born to be the King of all kings.

Shepherds, with dirt under the fingernails, grime in their brains and sheep drool on their robes who were invited to sing with the angels!

A song so loud and so triumphant that it broke through the coldness and darkness of a world in pain in order to pronounce, "Let there be joy!"

I am not intimately acquainted with the pain of your past nor do I know the stark reality of the Christmas that is knocking at your front door this year, however, this is what I do know about you and your life ...

You are loved by the God Who sent His Son into the darkness and confusion of the warzone of life this side of eternity.

The angels still invite modern day shepherds to sing ... to sing loudly ... to sing triumphantly!

Although your desire for "happy ever after" may be marred by the mess you have made of your life ... God still has the power to intervene because of Christmas!

And ... the message that the angel delivered to an incredulous virgin girl is still Heaven's message to you today ... nothing is impossible with God!

And so ... whatever circumstances you face today ... my prayer is that your life will be remembered as a lasting and genuine Christmas Carol because finally ... you understand ... you eternally comprehend what the best of times has always been about!

BIBLE READING

Luke 1:39-end

JOYFUL THOUGHTS TO PONDER

What is a happy Christmas memory that you have from years gone by?

What is a difficult Christmas memory from years gone by?

What can you do, this year, to make Christmas more joyful for those in your life?

_____

_____

_____

Merry Christmas... With Joy!

Have you ever treasured a memory so deeply in your soul that not only does your mind recall the facts of the moment but your heart also is instantly tied to the memory with intense and poignant feelings?

Such is the memory that I have of a December evening when I was only a miniature but perceptive 6 years old.

I attended kindergarten that morning in the one room schoolhouse that was just around the corner and up the street from the safe haven of my home. I lived in a century old home with my mom and dad, my older sister, a younger brother who loved to tease, a collie named Lassie and a white cat named Tinkerbell.

It was a snowy, wintery day in Western New York and I had spent the after school hours sledding with my older sister and with the "redheads" from across the street. My toes were nearly frostbitten from the time happily spent in the sub-freezing elements. My mother, after taking off all of my snow-caked outer garments at the door, handed me a fresh nightgown that had been warmed in the dryer. She then stood me on top of our old-fashioned register where the heat came blazing up from the basement furnace.

My mom was playing "The King Family Christmas Album" on our record player. I loved having Christmas music to listen to while I was slowly warming from the afternoon of frigid girlhood camaraderie!

Being unable to hold still, I revolved around in a small circle while the heat found its way to warm my numb toes, raw fingers and red nose.

My rotating turns offered instant and differing views of the world in which I was growing up. When facing one direction, I saw the piano sitting in the corner of the oversized room. Oh how I loved playing that piano!

As I slowly turned to face another direction, I saw the dining room table bedecked for Christmas in true 1960's fashion.

The third direction gave me a sweet look into my parents' bedroom and at their huge canopy bed that was the furniture masterpiece in our otherwise sparse home.

However, it is the fourth and final view that still tugs at my heart today, nearly 6 decades later.

As I completed my slow rotation, I was looking out of the front windows of my home and at the United States Post Office across the street. This particular day, I vividly recall that the snow was gently falling down around the little brown building that was truly no more than a glorified shack of governmental importance. The postmaster, Mr. Hawley, had strung lights around the roof and windows of the US Post Office located directly across the street from my girlhood home. My slow circle stopped the moment that I looked across the street at the obscure building.

As the King Family sang of city sidewalks, chestnuts roasting and finally about a Baby Boy, I stopped my circling and just stared, transfixed at the beauty of the brown building surrounded by Christmas lights.

I remember placing my hand on my chest because what I was experiencing in that moment was so wonderful and grand that it made my heart hurt. As I wiped the tears away from my no longer frozen cheeks, my mom walked into the room.

"Why, Carol!" she exclaimed. "Why are you crying? Are you not feeling well?"

I didn't even realize until that moment that there were tears on my cheeks. I responded,

"Mom ... it's all so beautiful. It makes my heart hurt."

The joy from my heart was leaking out of my eyes and down my innocent cheeks.

A little brown shingled building ... decorated with Christmas lights ... made my heart hurt.

And with repeating those words to you today ... I can still feel the glorious pain all over again.

Christmas is so beautiful ... so filled with wonder and glory ... that it makes my heart hurt to this very day.

When Christmas lights up the ordinary mundane of my feeble attempt at life, the raw marvel paints a picture of stunning impact. When viewed without the message of the manger, my life is truly just a shack of little significance and eternal obscurity.

However, when I dress my life in the majesty of the manger and with the glory of the angel's song it is then that I become who I was always made to be.

When the human hut of my life is changed by the purpose of the manger and by the star that led the way to His dear presence, I realize why my heart aches for something more than this world offers.

Even now ... the joy of Christmas is leaking out of my eyes and giving a sparkle to my cheeks. My now wizened heart hurts with the joy of it all.

Has the joy of Christmas changed you? Have you allowed the miracle of the manger to decorate the humdrum of your life?

My prayer for you this year is that you will take a moment out of the busyness ... and away from the craziness ... and observe with no distractions what the glory of Christmas is truly all about.

I hope that you will warm yourself with the joy of His presence.

I hope that you will hear the angels' song and that your heart will constrict in sheer and joyous pain.

I pray that you will have a moment when the joy of Christmas leaks out of your eyes and unto your face.

Your life was always meant to be more than a shack ... a hovel ... a hut of humanity. Your life was meant to be the showplace of Christmas every day of every year.

BIBLE READING

Matthew 1:18-25; Luke 2:1-20

JOYFUL THOUGHTS TO PONDER

If you could express the true meaning of Christmas in just one or two sentences, how would you describe it?

What are some of the customs of this season that have become a distraction for you?

What are some of the customs of this season that truly add to the joy and meaning for you?

_____

_____

_____

Something So Wonderful!

"It's the most wonderful time of the year!"

Now ... if that ain't the truth, I don't know what is!!

What?!!

(She said incredulously and with disbelief in her voice!)

You don't agree?!! You don't think that it's the most wonderful time of the year?!!

If you find yourself raging in religious disagreement with my heartfelt love of and for all things Christmas, then I hope that you will continue to read this simple and heartfelt chapter of devotion and Christmas joy. I hope that I can help you with your aversion to mistletoe, holiday cheer and with the decking of the holiday halls before you deck somebody!

It's true ... I am a Christmas-aholic. The resounding reason that I love Christmas so utterly and completely has nothing to do with overfed octogenarians in red suits trimmed with white fur, snowmen that dance at street corners or with cups filled with frothy holiday cheer.

The reason that my heart joyfully skips a beat at the mere thought of Christmas is because I am in love with the Savior of the world.

The reason that my eyes fill with tears every year the day after Thanksgiving is because I love babies. Especially a certain baby Boy born in a manger.

The reason that my heart sings with Heaven and with nature is because my world was dark and hopeless and it has now been filled to overflowing with the Light of the world and with the God of all hope.

The reason that I believe this season to be so earth-stoppingly spectacular is because I really do hear the song of the angels in my Christmas-infested heart.

> *"But the angel said to them, 'Do not be afraid, for behold, I bring you good news of great joy which shall be for all the people; for today in the city of David there has been born for you a Savior, Who is Christ the Lord."*

> —LUKE 2:10 & 11

The mistake that many Christian Scrooges make is that they confused the *magic* of the season with the *miracle* of the season. Truthfully, the *magic* of Christmas holds no eternal beauty or significance for me, either. It is the *miracle* of the season that causes my flesh to stand at attention and in amazement at the Gift that I have been given.

The magic of the season centers upon toy-making elves, flying reindeer with red noses and presents wrapped in silver and gold.

This is what I believe ... either the manger should be placed in the same category as elves, jolly old Saint Nicholas and flying reindeer ... or it is absolute, divine and eternal Truth.

Christmas is not about the holiday spirit that rushes toward us the day after Thanksgiving and compels us to shop, spend, and eat.

Christmas is about the Holy Spirit bringing peace and joy through a Baby Boy to the mess that we have made of planet earth.

Christmas is about the power of Heaven's reality invading one life.

It never ceases to amaze me that most of humanity pauses to celebrate the month of December. That's nothing short of miraculous! School children have concerts ... offices close their doors ... neighbors decorate with lights ... High School friends write long, newsy letters and send them in the mail ... and grocery stores offer treats offered at no other time of the year.

Why? It's because built into each one of us is the desire to celebrate! God made us to celebrate the miracle of Christmas! And, as believers, it is up to us to demonstrate to this lost, dark world exactly what they are celebrating! It is up to me and to you to reveal the joy of this season in extraordinary and miraculous ways!

It is up to you and I not to BECOME Scrooge but to OVERCOME Scrooge with the peace that was announced that night that stars exploded over the shepherds and their flocks.

It is up to us, with a smile on our faces, to shake our heads in agreement with the perky lyrics to songs that are sung only once a year, "It's the most wonderful time of the year!"

And then ... it is up to you and to me to live out the truth of this divine season ... He came so that my life could be wonderful.

God sent His Son so that I would have something to celebrate.

My entire life has been changed because of the most miraculous event in all of recorded history. God became man so that I could sing with the angels a song so victorious and hopeful that the world must listen.

It really is the most wonderful time of the year, isn't it?

BIBLE READING
Matthew 2:1-12

JOYFUL THOUGHTS TO PONDER
What is the best Christmas gift that you have ever received?

What is the best Christmas gift that you have ever given?

Other than the Baby Jesus, who is your favorite character in the Christmas story and why?

_____

_____

_____

Auld Lang Syne

Happy "Almost" New Year, my friend!

It's the time of year for wearing crazy party hats … for blowing ridiculous noise-makers … for counting down the seconds of the waning year … for lifting a toast or two … and for making unattainable, elusive, impracticable resolutions.

January 1 is the one day of the calendar year when making a new start truly seems possible, isn't it?! The slate is clean and the calendar page is empty. Dreams of heretofore unreached goals seem sure and certain.

Every day is a gift from God but there is something bigger and more spectacular about the gift of an unfolding and exciting New Year.

Regardless of marital status, socioeconomic level, health concerns, behavior of children, academic degrees, stamps in a passport, or the tidiness of one's home, we have all been given the exact same gift.

12 months of undiscovered possibilities.

52 weeks of being thankful.

365 days to unwrap with joy.

8,760 hours of His presence in our lives.

525,600 minutes of miracles!

What will you do with this rare and extraordinary gift that you have been given?

Will you make a decision to lose 50 pounds only to feel like a failure by January 12?

Will you determine to travel the world this year when you know that would take the financial provision that only winning the lottery provides?

Have you resolved to spend less ... eat less ... weigh less ... and work less?

Is it within your heart to love more ... live more ... enjoy more ... and sing more?

What will you do with these 12 untouched months?

Rather than making futile goals that will only frustrate the delight of life out of every day, I'd like to make a few suggestions that will enable you to wring the joy out of every day in the coming year. Because, after all, that is why God gives us 24 hours in a day ... it is to experience His presence where there is always fullness of joy!

NEW YEAR'S SUGGESTIONS FOR THE COMING YEAR

1. Don't allow one complaint to come out of your lips! Your mouth was made for the sole purpose of praising the Lord and encouraging others. Don't complain about the weather, about politics, about the price of gas or about your mom! Use your tongue for the purpose for which it was created ... to encourage others and to worship the Lord! Just think ... by the end of this year you may have lost your ability to whine and complain! How amazing is that?!!

2. Memorize one Scripture verse every month. That might not sound like a lot ... but just think ... at the end of this year you will have memorized 12 new Bible verses that will have enlarged your life exponentially!

3. 12 people! What 12 people has God assigned you to in over the next 12 calendar months? Ask God to give you the names of 12 friends, family members or acquaintances who may desperately need your prayers, your encouragement, your attention and your love. Just think ... when December 31st rolls around again, you will have changed 12 people's lives for all of eternity!

4. Read at least one book every month this year. Ask people whom

you admire for a suggestion of a book or two to read this year. Just think ... at the end of 12 months ... you could be a 12 times smarter and wiser "you" than you were during the past 12 months!

5. Become important in the life of a child. So often, our human desire is to rub shoulders with the rich, famous and influential when it is children who actually deserve our attention. Have some little girls over for an afternoon tea party ... play kickball with the neighborhood kids ... take a group of middle school boys to a baseball game ... teach Sunday School ... offer to babysit for a single mom. Children are our greatest natural resource and have more treasure to add to your life this year than do silver and gold. Time spent with a child is never wasted time. Just think ... at the end of the coming year ... there will be the imprint of new little fingerprints all over your heart.

6. Read your Bible every day. The Bible has the power to bring out the best in you, to deliver wisdom to your life, to usher peace into your days and to enable you to hear the voice of God! What a divine possibility! Imagine it! By the time a new year dawns again ... you might be thinking, talking and acting a whole lot more like God simply because you chose to read the Bible!

7. Keep a prayer journal this year. Write down the prayer requests that are shared at church, on Facebook, at Bible Study and from the hearts of your friends. Don't just pray for yourself and for your personal concerns but pray for the people who are placed in your life by God. By the end of the next 52 short weeks, you will have an entire journal filled up with the miracles that prayer has accomplished! You and God will have partnered in miracles that are much too amazing for words!

8. Do something kind for someone else every day. Say an encouraging word to someone in your life every single day. Do not let one day pass by without reaching out in kindness and in encouragement to friends, family members and even to complete strangers! What heavenly fun this will be! Pay for someone else's coffee ... write an encouraging note ... send dinner to someone who is in a health struggle ... give that single mom at church a $20 bill ... take donuts to the office ... call your best friend from childhood and reconnect. Just think ... when the next New Year

commences … you will look back at this year and realize that when you give away kindness and encouragement that you are the one who is living a rich life indeed!

9. Don't waste one day in discouragement, anger or unforgiveness. Remind yourself that each new day is a gift from God with the expanse of Heaven at its core. Appreciate each day for the miracle that it is and partner with God in liberally splashing the joy of His presence everywhere you go! Can you even imagine the joy that will fill your heart when January dawns again? Your life will be more than wonderful! Your life will be wonderful not because of things or stuff … not because of a number on the bathroom scale or due to the extravagant bottom line in your checking account … but you will be living a truly wonderful life because your life smacks of the purposes and plans of God!

Happy New Year, my friend! Make it a great one!

BIBLE READING

Lamentations 3:21-26; Philippians 3:7-14

JOYFUL THOUGHTS TO PONDER

What is the greatest miracle or answer to prayer you have observed during the past calendar year? Share it with someone today?

Make a list of 12 people who need your kindness and encouragement this year.

What are the things for which you are praying in the coming year?

What are you looking forward to with joy in the coming year?

_____

_____

_____

Refined
Finding Joy in the Midst of the Fire
by Carol Burton McLeod

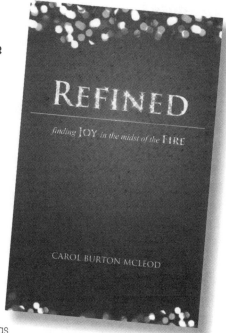

Why? Well-known author Carol Burton McLeod has found answers to these questions:

- Why do we go through hard times?

- Why do the beloved children of a merciful, compassionate Father have to face tragedies and heartbreaking circumstances?

- Where is God when these things are happening?

Refined shows how God provides comfort and encouragement for people who are broken and disappointed with the circumstances and events of life.

Refined provides the reader with practical, helpful, and hopeful insights.

Refined shows how to find joy even when your world is falling apart.

Refined helps the reader find and experience God's great love, peace, and joy.

CAROL BURTON MCLEOD is a public speaker who empowers others with passionate and practical biblical messages. She has written four other books: *No More Ordinary, Holy Estrogen!, The Rooms of a Woman's Heart,* and *Defiant Joy.* Her devotionals are featured on YouVersion, and she is a weekly writer for Ministry Today magazine. Her daily radio show, "Defiant Joy! Radio" is available in several national markets, including Sirius 131 Family Talk XM radio. A 1977 graduate of Oral Roberts University, she is married to her college sweetheart, Craig, who is the Senior Pastor of Life Church near Buffalo.

ISBN: 978-1-61036-144-6
TPB / 216 pages

No More Ordinary
Living the life you were made for
by Carol Burton McLeod

CAROL McLEOD partners with the Word of God and the lives of victorious believers to show you how to obtain and maintain the full and wonderful life that God wants you to have. Your life can be extraordinary!

Learn how to tackle life with zest in spite of the circumstances. Discover how to live the life you were made for, as you learn what made the difference for people like Corrie ten Boom, Robert LeTourneau, Ruth Bell Graham, Hank and Betty Stam, Susannah Wesley, and many others.

The author writes: "This Heaven-guaranteed, extraordinary, too-good-to-be-true life starts the instant a sinner admits his or her need for a Savior. Life with a capital 'L' begins the moment that you make the miraculous decision to enter into a partnership with the Man whose very identity is known as Life himself!"

This book is a no-compromise, how-to-get-there-from-here manual that will take you out of the humdrum and mediocrity of this earthly existence and take you into an abundant life that is full of joy!

CAROL BURTON MCLEOD says, "I am just a girl who is head over heels in love with Jesus. I am passionately addicted to His Word, and I find all the joy I need as I spend time in His presence." She describes herself as a Christmas-holic, and she is very fond of chocolate and enjoys a good read. She doesn't like cleaning her house and has become an expert in carry-out dinners. She hates to shop, loves to jog, and somehow finds time in her busy life to hang out with small children. She is the kind of woman you could laugh with over lunch, cry with over disappointment, and shout over with victory.

ISBN: 978-1-61036-120-0
TPB / 216 pages

If you are interested in having Carol McLeod speak at your conference Women's Retreat or event, please contact us:

Just Joy! Ministries
PO Box 1294
Orchard Park, NY 14127

(by phone) 855-569-5433
(by email) info@justjoyministries.com
For more information, visit our website at www.JustJoyMinistries.com

Follow Carol McLeod on Social Media

 Carol McLeod Bible Teacher and Author

 @justjoyceo

 @justjoyceo

 Carol McLeod Channel

YouVersion™

21 Days to Beat Depression
Joy to YOUR World
Holy Emotions
For the Joy Set Before Him
She Is ... Mom
Refined - Finding Joy in the Midst
of the Fire
Extraordinary Ordinary
Just Joy! Bible Reading Strategy

Listen daily at 2:30 pm (ET) on SiriusXM Family Talk Channel 131 or check our website to see the station information for your town!

Podcasts are also available on the Charisma Podcast Network as well as the Just Joy Ministries website.

Books and CD/DVD Teachings are available on the Just Joy! website
www.JustJoyMinistries.com